KOREAN COOKING

EXPLORE ONE OF THE ORIENT'S GREATEST CULINARY SECRETS

HILAIRE WALDEN

Quantum Books

A QUANTUM BOOK

Published by Eagle Editions Ltd
11 Heathfield
Royston
Hertfordshire SG8 5BW

This edition printed 2003

ISBN 1-86160-633-8

QUMKOR

This book is produced by
Quantum Publishing Ltd
6 Blundell Street
London N7 9BH

Typeset in Great Britain by
Central Southern Typesetters, Eastbourne
Manufactured in China by
Regent Publishing Services Ltd.
Printed in Singapore by
Star Standard Industries (Pte) Ltd.

There are at least two widely used forms for transliterating written Korean (even in Korea inconsistencies can occur). The main accepted form is the McCane-Reichauer and it is this that has been followed, as far as possible, in this book.

ACKNOWLEDGEMENTS
Pictures courtesy of Korea National Tourism Corporation (pages 6, 8, 15, 36, 39, 42, 49, 61, 65, 77, 91, 92, 101, 114, 119)
The publisher would like to thank Také Ltd, London, for providing props for photography

CONTENTS

INTRODUCTION

Korea is rarely thought of as a beautiful country, yet it has superb scenery – plunging waterfalls, verdant paddy fields, cedar forests, Mongolian desert and wide, sea-lapped beaches. Its walled villages have reddish-brown, tiled roofs of locally made stone. Many of the old traditions still survive and in country areas, the men still wear stove-pipe hats and baggy trousers tied at the ankles. In the cities the old rubs shoulders with the new. Seoul, the capital of South Korea, is a high-rise city criss-crossed with multiple highways which overshadow walled temples and old royal palaces. In the six-storey East Gate Market over 15,000 shoppers a day visit walkways where cooked pigs' heads, squid and fresh chickens are sold beside quilted cushions and bolts of coloured silk.

Over the centuries Korea has been the focus of much aggressive attention from her neighbours, and each wave of intruders has left a mark on Korean cuisine.

As early as BC 100 Chinese colonies were burgeoning around the peninsula to the extent that Silla, in the south of ancient Korea, called itself with some pride, "Little China". Ancient Korea, in fact, comprised three kingdoms: Koguryo in the North; Paekche and Silla in the South. They were all culturally advanced and had a centralized government, royal courts, nobility and a class system. A unified country was established after the kingdom of Silla, assisted by the Chinese, conquered first Paekche and then Koguryo. In this new country there were five provincial capitals administered by a sophisticated civil service. There were also splendid grand palaces, elaborate temples and tombs and imposing monuments.

Then, in the thirteenth century, Genghis Khan's Mongol hordes swept over the country.

BELOW *An open market. A rich variety of grains and pulses is available.*

In 1876 Korea concluded a trade treaty with Japan, much to the alarm of China. Europeans had started to arrive after the mid-seventeenth century and after the signing of the Japanese treaty others were agreed with European countries and America.

In 1910, Japan annexed Korea and retained rule over her until after the end of World War II. From China and Japan Korea adopted the principle of the five flavours – sweet, sour, hot, salty and bitter – and the practice of spending more time cutting, slicing and dicing ingredients, especially vegetables, than cooking them. The Korean version of the wok, the *sot*, is also a legacy of the Chinese and the presence of the Mongols is still apparent in the predeliction for table-top cooking.

Topography and climate determine to a large extent the foods naturally available and the type of dishes that are cooked. Being surrounded on three sides by water, fish is important in Korean cuisine. There is an almost endless supply of fish and shellfish – red snapper, skate, sole, pollack, tuna, herring, cod, croaker, horse mackerel, corvina, oysters, prawns, shrimps, clams, abalone, mussels, sea snails and sea cucumber, to name just some. The cold, deep Sea of Japan off the east coast provides the deepwater varieties such as squid and cuttlefish while the shallower Yellow Sea that stretches away towards China supplies those that thrive in warmer waters.

The shores are also a source of sea vegetables which the Koreans have enjoyed eating for centuries, for example, kelp, laver and seaweed.

The mountains that occupy much of the country provide a selection of wild vegetables, mushrooms, herbs and roots. The lowlands and plains of the south support large areas of agriculture. Modern food production techniques have enabled South Korea to increase the cultivation and yields of vegetables, grains and fruits and today enough rice and corn are grown to satisfy the country's needs. Vegetables like sweet and white potatoes, carrots, soya beans, white radishes, Chinese cabbage, spring onions and red peppers, flavourful fruits such as apples, plums, peaches, grapes and luscious strawberries, nuts and grains, are cultivated. Semi-tropical Cheju Island supplies tangerines and oranges.

As you travel further south the food becomes hotter, spicier and more salty. Unusually for an eastern Asian country, beef is the most popular meat (pork and chicken usually reign supreme). This liking for beef is said to be a legacy of Mongolian ancestors. Mongol tribes first migrated south from what is now Manchuria in prehistoric times but it was the warring, pillaging, thirteenth-century Mongol armies who decided the best place to raise cattle was on the rich pastures of Cheju Island. The practice continues today. Now, the pastures are divided into American-style ranges, some as large as 81,000 hectares (200,000 acres), and the cattle are just as likely to be Western Charolais, Aberdeen Angus and Hereford as local breeds.

Korea has hot summers with plentiful rain (ideal for much agriculture, particularly rice) but bitterly cold winters. These have given rise to the Korean tradition of preserving fish and vegetables to provide food during the lean months. All manner of fish and shellfish, such as anchovies, shrimps, oysters, pollack, cuttlefish and octopus are pickled, salted and dried, while vegetables are pickled and turned into *kimchi*. Every autumn, in the country vast

ABOVE *Popular at every mealtime, Kimchis are prepared in vast quantities.*

amounts of vegetables are harvested to make large batches of a wide range of different *kimchis*. These are then packed into enormous earthenware jars that are buried in the ground outside and left until required. Although the necessity for so much preservation does not exist nowadays, Koreans still make their traditional preserves because they enjoy eating them so much. Also, salted shrimps and oysters are a common addition to *kimchi* as they increase the mineral content and enrich the flavour; they dissolve during the fermentation and do not give a fishy taste.

Every house will also have its *jang* terrace. In the country this will be a stone area outside but in towns and cities a balcony or flat roof will have to suffice. On the *jang* terrace stand large earthenware jars of basic ingredients used in every Korean kitchen – *kanjang* (soy sauce), *twoenjang* (fermented soya bean paste) and *kochujang* (chilli bean paste). Cooks used to ferment their own beans to make these condiments but now the sauces are usually bought ready-made.

Social factors also influence who eats what, and how they eat it. As Korea has a long-established hierarchical system there is a deep-seated division between the elaborate, rich and more sophisticated foods of the courts and upper classes like *Shinsollo* and *Kujolpan* (see page 26) and the robust, hearty fare of the people.

Food is associated with the many Korean festivals. Rice cakes and taro soup are served for the New Year, and chrysanthemum cakes and wine for the ninth day of the ninth month. Fruit, wine and cakes are taken on a special date to ancestors' graves, and on its first birthday a child sits amidst biscuits, rice cakes and fruit. The sixty-first birthday is also cause for celebration. Sixty is traditionally regarded as the average life-span, so to have survived one year more is an accomplishment to warrant a grand celebratory feast.

EATING KOREAN-STYLE

As in other Far Eastern countries, such as China, Thailand and Japan, Koreans sit around a low table to eat. Every person has their own rice bowl, traditionally made of brass and usually lidded. Long, pencil-thin metal chopsticks are used for eating, with a metal spoon for soups.

All the dishes for a meal are served at once and often, particularly for dinner, the main meal of the day, there will be quite a few. A simple family dinner, for example, might include some 20 *panchan* (side dishes) containing a tempting array of *namuls* (seasoned raw or lightly cooked vegetables); *nibles* such as dried vegetables and shrimps, salted fish, roast seaweed; dipping sauces and *kimchi* (at least one type of these is essential and preferably there should be three or four). Soup is also an essential element of every meal, and there are also likely to be some *jon* (flour- and egg-coated fried vegetables). Even more substantial fish, meat and poultry dishes are served in what would be considered small amounts in the West. With such variety on offer large portions of any one thing are unnecessary.

Lunch is a lighter meal of noodles or rice mixed with vegetables, or another grain or beans for protein. Breakfast is traditionally almost as large as dinner but, nowadays, it tends to be lighter. Even so, there will be at least rice, soup and *kimchi*. In the cities, smaller Western-style breakfasts are becoming more popular.

Slurping while eating is considered an indication that the food is being enjoyed and a good belch afterwards is a sign of having eaten well. However, blowing the nose at table is a grave social misdemeanour (an offender is demoted to the status of a *sangnom* – an unperson).

EQUIPMENT

As it is the cuisine of country people, preparing Korean food requires only simple, limited equipment and little in the way of complicated skills. It does, however, take a long time to prepare a traditional Korean meal because it contains so many different dishes.

The traditional Korean kitchen is situated at or below ground. Cooking is done on a two- or four-burner hob that is fuelled by anthracite. Pipes run from the range under the floor of the living areas of houses to provide a system of central heating.

RICE COOKER Because of the amount of rice that is eaten, city dwellers now use electric rice cookers as they cook rice perfectly every time and will keep the rice hot.

KNIVES Preparing Korean food takes much time-consuming chopping and slicing, so good-quality sharp knives are most important. A food processor, mandoline slicer or grater can be used and, for wafer-thin slices, a potato peeler. A sharp knife is also necessary for slicing and scoring meat and poultry.

HANDS Koreans often use their hands for mixing, for example, ingredients for a marinade, and for beating eggs as less air is incorporated.

TABLE-TOP COOKER Koreans are very fond of cooking food at table. For this, small table-top burners fuelled by small butane gas canisters are often used. Metal grids are used for cooking the food directly over the flame.

SHINSOLLO A special bronze or brass pot is used for preparing the dish of the same name. The pot has a central funnel in which hot charcoal is placed to keep the food hot.

THE FLAVOURS OF KOREAN COOKING

Garlic, chillies, ginger, spring onions, sesame oil and sesame seeds – these provide the staple and stable character of Korean food and at least one will appear in nearly every dish. In addition there are other ingredients essential to Korean cooking, some of which follow.

BEAN CURD

White, milky, thick custard-like bean curd is made from soya beans, and is high in protein and low in fat. Bean curd is widely used in Korean cooking; it is served on its own after being sautéd, deep-fried or braised, added to soups, casseroles and braised dishes.

Fresh bean curd can be made at home (see page 114) or bought from healthfood and ethnic shops. Bean curd usually comes in three textures – soft, medium and firm. It is best eaten on the day it is bought, or made, but may be stored in a container, covered by cold water and refrigerated for 2–3 days; change the water every day.

BEAN CURD

CHILLIES

CHILLIES

Ripe, red chillies are used in Korea. There are many different varieties of chilli and each variety has its own flavour and hotness; size is not an infallible guide to hotness, but generally the larger the chilli the less intense the heat. Chopping a chilli increases the amount of "fire" in a dish, as does including the seeds. Chillies add flavour as well as hotness so, for a milder dish, instead of reducing the number of chillies used, leave the chillies whole, if possible, and discard the seeds. Chillies are also painstakingly cut into fine shreds for using as a garnish in Korean cooking.

Chillies should be handled carefully as they contain a substance that can irritate the skin. If you have a cut, bruise or lesion on your hands, or your skin is sensitive, wear thin rubber gloves when preparing chillies.

CHILLI POWDER

Korean chilli powder is among the best in the world. It is relatively mild, a glowing carmine colour and coarsely pounded. It tastes somewhat like a cross between paprika and cayenne pepper (which can be used as a substitute if necessary). It is added to dishes with generosity, not only flavouring them and adding "heat", but giving them a characteristic glorious vibrant colour.

GARLIC

Garlic goes into a great many savoury dishes. Koreans like their garlic to have impact – in stir-fry dishes it is added at the end, not the beginning of the cooking (the pungency diminishes during cooking) and cloves may be pounded, then finely chopped, to release the maximum flavour. Koreans also eat whole, peeled cloves – dishes of them are put on restaurant tables to be nibbled neat or cooked on a table-top grill. Most Korean markets and supermarkets sell ready-peeled garlic.

GARLIC

GINGER

GINGER

Ginger is a very popular addition to many Korean dishes. Choose plump fresh ginger so there is a high proportion of flesh to skin, and make sure it feels firm and has a shiny skin.

KIMCHI

Kimchi is the spicy national pickle. It is ubiquitous. Not only is it considered a vital part of every meal, including breakfast, but is added to soups, stews, stir-fries and pancakes. You do not have to make your own (see pages 40–64) as bottles of *kimchi* can be bought from Korean grocers and supermarkets.

There are many different types of *kimchi* – in the Seoul museum devoted entirely to *kimchi*, there are 160 different versions, such as Chinese leaf, white radish, cucumber, stuffed cucumber, garlic, Chinese turnip and onion.

KOCHUJANG

Kochujang is Korea's red, spicy version of a chilli bean paste. It is an essential seasoning and serves as a cross between a relish and a spice. *Kochujang* is added to meats that are to be stir-fried, stews and dips, and served in small bowls as a sweet, spicy, hot relish.

In every household in Korea there is a tall earthenware jar of thick, red *kochujang* – its preparation is lengthy and elaborate, using glutinous rice powder or barley mixed with malt, then cooking it slowly to a smooth, thick paste. This is mixed with fermented chilli powder, soy bean powder and salt.

Kochujang can also be bought ready-made in jars in Korea. In the West it is only available from Korean supermarkets. An improvised version can be made at home (see page 69), or you can use Chinese chilli bean paste available at most supermarkets.

CELLOPHANE NOODLES

NOODLES

Cellophane noodles are also known as bean thread or transparent noodles. They are made from ground mung beans and are clear-white, fine, dried strands that are so tough they are almost impossible to cut. They are sold in bundles and need to be soaked for 10–15 minutes before cooking. After cooking cellophane noodles become soft, slippery and gelatinous.

Buckwheat noodles Korean buckwheat noodles, *son myon*, are very thin dried noodles. Japanese *shoba* noodles are also made from buckwheat but are fatter; Japanese *somen* noodles or Italian vermicelli or capellini are nearer in size to Korean buckwheat noodles but they are made from wheat flour.

RICE VINEGAR

RICE VINEGAR

For the recipes in this book use Japanese rice vinegar, which is lighter and milder than Chinese brands. White wine vinegar can be substituted, or dilute 3 parts white distilled vinegar with 1 part water; if the recipe does not include sugar, add a small pinch.

RICE WINE

Rice wine is a light, slightly sweet wine. Use dry sherry if it is not available.

SESAME OIL

SESAME OIL

In Korea, sesame oil is used as a flavouring as well as for cooking. The sesame oil used in Korea is made from toasted sesame seeds so has an amber colour and nutty sesame flavour. As it therefore provides a characteristic flavour as well as colour, using pale sesame oil instead will not give authentic-tasting dishes. Keep sesame oil in a cool, dark place.

BLACK AND WHITE SESAME SEEDS

SESAME SEEDS

Sesame seeds are used in such quantities that they are often bought by the tubful in the autumn soon after harvesting, when the price is at its lowest. Small quantities of sesame seeds are roasted at a time in a heavy, dry pan then lightly crushed with salt (see page 22). These are added to sauces, marinades, dips and salads as well as braised dishes. Black sesame seeds have a more pronounced, and slightly more bitter taste than white sesame seeds. They are also used in Chinese and Japanese cookery.

SEA VEGETABLES

Dried kelp is a green, calcium-rich sea vegetable resembling large, long leaves. Called *tasima* in Korean, it is also known by its Japanese name, *konbu* or *kombu*. It is available either folded or cut into small pieces. A fine white salty deposit forms on the surface; this should not be washed off as the flavour of kelp is near the surface. Instead, wipe with a damp cloth just before using.

KELP AND WAKAME

Dried laver is also well known by its Japanese name, *nori*; the Korean name is *kim*. It is thin, crisp and vitamin- and mineral-packed. There are many varieties and qualities, from dark green to purplish black and from medium-priced to expensive; price is usually a good guide to quality. Like dried kelp, dried laver is available from healthfood shops as well as ethnic shops and is generally sold in sheets about 18 x 20cm/7 x 8in. Store dried laver in an air-tight container.

Before dried laver is eaten it is passed over a flame several times until it becomes crisp (see page 29). It may then be eaten as it is or crumbled over noodle or rice dishes.

Dried seaweed A green type of seaweed, often known by its Japanese name of *wakame*, is used in Korea in soups and stews, and dressed with a vinegar dressing in salads. When dried, *wakame* darkens and is sold in small packets in healthfood and ethnic shops. Before using, it should be soaked for about 30 minutes, after which time some of its former colour returns and it becomes fairly slippery.

RICE

Korean rice is a medium- to short-grain variety that becomes sticky when cooked (see page 102). It is available from Korean grocers and supermarkets but if you are not able to buy it, substitute Japanese rice.

RICE

LIGHT AND DARK SOYA BEAN PASTE

SOYA BEAN PASTE

Soya bean paste is made from fermented soya bean cakes, pepper and salt. This thick brown paste has a pungent, characteristic flavour. Japanese miso can be used as a substitute.

SOY SAUCE

SOY SAUCE

Soy sauce is an essential flavouring and seasoning. Light, medium and dark soy sauces are available; light versions tend to be the thinnest and most salty. Japanese soy sauce (medium) has been used for all of the recipes in this book.

SPRING ONIONS

A variety of shapes and sizes of spring onion is found in Korea, but the most common are larger than typical Western spring onions. Use the plumpest you can find for the recipes in this book (Middle Eastern shops often sell fatter, plumper spring onions).

CHINESE MUSHROOMS AND WOOD EAR FUNGUS

CHINESE MUSHROOMS

These are black or brown dried mushrooms. Long ago the Chinese discovered that drying them intensifies their flavour. They should be soaked in water for about 20 minutes, then squeezed to get rid of the salt. Wood Ear Fungus is another form of dried mushroom, valued for its subtle, delicate flavour and slightly crunchy "bite". When soaked, it expands to five times its dried size.

Soups are an important component of every proper Korean meal, even breakfast, but soup is not eaten at the beginning of the meal, as in the West; instead it is served with the other dishes. Although traditional Korean meals do not feature a first course (all the dishes are served at once), there are recipes that are suitable for serving at the beginning of Western-style meals. Koreans are very fond of nibbling, especially when they are drinking; the abundant drinking houses (*suljip*) have an array of snacks on offer to their customers in the hope of increasing the drinking rate, in a similar way to Spanish *tapas* bars. These snacks can also be served at home to accompany drinks, instead of crisps and peanuts, or for a light first course.

SPINACH SOUP

Shikumchiguk

This is a favourite soup throughout South Korea.

SERVES 3-4

150g/5oz chicken breast, thinly sliced and cut into 2.5cm/1in cubes
3 spring onions, finely chopped
2 garlic cloves, chopped
2 tbsp soy sauce
1½ tsp sesame seeds
freshly ground black pepper
1½ tbsp vegetable oil
1.25 litres/2¼pt Korean Chicken Stock (see below)
350g/12oz fresh spinach, trimmed and shredded
sesame oil for sprinkling

❖ Mix the chicken with the spring onions, garlic, soy sauce, sesame seeds and plenty of pepper. Leave for 30 minutes.

❖ Heat the vegetable oil in a large saucepan, add the chicken mixture and fry until browned. Add the chicken stock and heat until just simmering. Simmer very gently for about 25 minutes until the chicken is tender.

❖ Add the spinach and cook for a further 2–5 minutes until the spinach is tender. Adjust the seasonings; if the liquid has reduced too much, add hot water as necessary.

❖ Serve sprinkled with sesame oil.

KOREAN CHICKEN STOCK

Dack Kukmul

The garlic cloves can be left whole, cut into halves or chopped according to how pronounced you want the flavour to be.

MAKES ABOUT 1.2 LITRES/2PT

1 chicken carcass, preferably with skin, or about 675–900g/1½–2lb raw or cooked chicken trimmings, bones and skin
3 thin slices of fresh ginger
2 garlic cloves (optional)
2 spring onions, white and some green parts split lengthways

❖ Put the chicken into a large saucepan, add 1.75 litres/3pt water and bring slowly to the boil. Skim the scum from the surface. Add the garlic, ginger and split spring onions. Cover and simmer for about 3 hours.

❖ Strain through a sieve lined with muslin. Leave until cold then put in the refrigerator until set. Remove the fat from the surface of the stock. Cover and keep in the refrigerator for up to 4 days; boil every other day.

SEAWEED SOUP

Miyoguk

Wrap the meat and put it in the freezer for about 35 minutes to make cutting it into strips easier. *Wakame* is the Japanese name for a green type of seaweed available dried in packets from healthfood and ethnic shops.

SERVES 6

115g/4oz dried *wakame*, soaked for at least 30 minutes
1.5 litres/2½pt fish or beef stock
1 bunch spring onions, white and some green parts chopped
1 tbsp sesame oil
1 garlic clove, crushed and finely chopped
175g/6oz lean tender beef, cut into fine strips
soy sauce
toasted sesame seeds for garnish

❖ Drain the wakame and cut it into strips.

❖ Pour the stock into a saucepan, add the spring onions and bring to the boil. Lower the heat so the stock simmers gently. Heat the oil in a frying-pan, add the garlic and beef and stir-fry for about 2 minutes. Add to the stock together with the wakame. Add soy sauce to taste and heat through. Serve garnished with toasted sesame seeds.

CHICKEN SOUP WITH CLAMS AND SPINACH

Takguk

Shellfish and poultry have a natural affinity. Here, chicken and clams are combined with great success, and the union is enhanced by spinach.

SERVES 4

16 clams
1 tbsp vegetable oil
2 garlic cloves, crushed and finely chopped
1½–2 tsp finely chopped fresh ginger
3 spring onions, white and some green parts chopped
1 chicken breast, cut into very fine strips
900ml/1½pt Korean Chicken Stock (see page 16)
350g/12oz fresh spinach, chopped
1½ tsp sesame oil
salt and freshly ground black pepper

❖ Scrub the clams and rinse them under running cold water.

❖ Heat the vegetable oil in a saucepan, add the garlic, ginger, spring onions and chicken and stir-fry for 30 seconds. Add the chicken stock and bring to the boil. Simmer for 5 minutes.

❖ Add the clams, return to the boil and simmer for 3–5 minutes until the clam shells open; discard any that remain closed. Stir in the spinach, simmer for 1–2 minutes then remove the pan from the heat. Add the sesame oil and season to taste.

White Radish Soup ▶

WHITE RADISH SOUP

Kakguk

This warming, soothing soup is usually served for breakfast.

SERVES 4-6

16 dried Chinese mushrooms, soaked in hot water for 30 minutes
1.5 litres/2½pt Korean Chicken Stock (see page 16)
450g/1lb white radish, diced
275g/10oz mung beansprouts
1 tsp soy sauce
½ tsp sugar
freshly ground black pepper

❖ Remove the mushrooms from the soaking water. Strain the water and reserve.

❖ Remove and discard the stalks from the mushrooms. Thinly slice the caps and put into a large saucepan with the stock. Bring to the boil and add the white radish. Cover the saucepan and simmer gently for about 10 minutes until the white radish is tender.

❖ Add the beansprouts, return to the boil, cover again and simmer for a further 3–4 minutes. Add the soy sauce, sugar and pepper.

DUMPLING SOUP

Manduguk

Korean dumpling soup is nothing like a British soup with dumplings but contains small dumplings filled with water chestnuts, pork and chicken, like Chinese *dim sum*.

SERVES 6

I carrot, chopped
I onion, chopped
I garlic clove, chopped
6 water chestnuts, chopped
115g/4oz lean pork
115g/4oz chicken
115g/4oz cooked, peeled prawns
2 tbsp soy sauce
I tbsp sesame oil
pinch of Korean chilli powder, or cayenne pepper mixed with paprika
30 wonton wrappers
1.75 litres/3pt Korean Chicken Stock (see page 16)
spring onions, chopped, to garnish

❖ Put the vegetables and three-quarters of the pork, chicken and prawns in a food processor. Dice the remaining pork, chicken and prawns. Add the soy sauce, sesame oil and a pinch of Korean chilli powder, or cayenne pepper mixed with paprika, to the food processor and mix to a smooth paste.

❖ Spoon a little of the vegetable mixture into each wonton wrapper, wet the edges and draw together to make a neat bundle. Pinch the edges together to seal.

❖ Bring the stock to the boil in a saucepan, add the dumplings and diced pork, chicken and prawns. Simmer for 8–10 minutes. Garnish with spring onion before serving.

COLD BUCKWHEAT NOODLE SOUP

Naengmyon

This soup is almost a meal in itself. Because of the number of elements which have to be prepared separately it may appear to be a complicated recipe, but, in fact, each vegetable is simple to prepare and all of them can be done in advance.

SERVES 4

225g/8oz buckwheat noodles
1.2 litres/2pt Korean Chicken Stock (see page 16)
1 tsp sesame oil
½ long cucumber, thinly sliced
salt
1½ tsp rice vinegar
pinch of sugar
pinch of Korean chilli powder, or cayenne pepper mixed with paprika
2 hard-boiled eggs, shelled and thinly sliced
8 pieces of white radish, cut into thin strips
½ Korean (Asian) pear, peeled, cored and thinly sliced
225ml/8fl oz liquid from white radish
selection of Dipping Sauces (see sesame page 58, vinegar page 32 and ginger page 35) to serve

❖ Cook the noodles according to the instructions on the packet. Drain and rinse under running cold water. Drain well then put into a bowl and toss with 115ml/4fl oz of the stock, and the sesame oil.

❖ Put the cucumber slices in a colander and toss with salt. Leave for 1 hour. Rinse the cucumber well, drain and dry thoroughly on paper towels. Mix with the rice vinegar, sugar and chilli powder, or cayenne pepper mixed with paprika.

❖ Divide the noodles between four dishes. Pour one quarter of the remaining stock into each dish. Arrange a few neatly overlapping slices of egg around the top of each pile of noodles. Surround with slightly overlapping vegetable and pear slices.

BEEF SOUP

Mou-kuk

Korean turnips are large and round. Substitute two small round turnips if the Korean variety are not available.

SERVES 6

750g/1½lb braising beef
1 Korean turnip or 2 small round turnips, peeled
2½ tbsp sesame oil
2 garlic cloves, crushed and finely chopped
4 spring onions, white and some green parts chopped
1 tsp sugar
1 tbsp Crushed Toasted Sesame Seeds (see below)
1½ tbsp Korean chilli powder, or cayenne pepper mixed with paprika
1½ tbsp soy sauce
salt (optional)

❖ Put the beef and turnip in a saucepan with 1.5 litres/2½pt water. Bring to the boil, skim the scum from the surface, then cover and simmer gently for 1½–2 hours until the meat is very tender. Remove from the heat and leave the beef and turnip to cool in the liquid.

❖ Skim the fat from the surface of the liquid and remove the beef and turnip. Thinly slice the turnip and finely chop the beef.

❖ Heat the sesame oil in a saucepan, add the garlic and spring onions and fry for 2 minutes. Stir in the beef, turnip, sugar, sesame seeds, chilli powder, or cayenne mixed with paprika, and soy sauce and cook for a couple of minutes. Add to the stock and heat through, 5 minutes.

CRUSHED TOASTED SESAME SEEDS

Prepare the quantity of these that is appropriate to the amount of Korean cooking you are going to do (it is easy to increase or halve the recipe) and keep them in a screw-top jar in a cool, dark place.

50g/2oz sesame seeds
2 tsp salt

❖ Heat a small, heavy frying-pan over a medium-low heat. Add the sesame seeds and stir until they darken a shade and give off a toasted, nutty aroma.

❖ Crush the seeds with the salt in a pestle and mortar. Keep in a screw-top jar.

MUNG BEAN PANCAKES

Pindaetuk

Pindaetuk are a popular street snack but they are also made in restaurants and homes for celebratory occasions such as birthdays, weddings and New Year. The street versions are usually a thick, approximately 18cm/7in, round whereas when cooked in restaurants or homes they are thinner and smaller.

MAKES ABOUT 8 PANCAKES

185g/6½oz whole mung beans, soaked for 10 hours
2 tbsp short-grain rice, washed and soaked (see page 102)
50g/2oz red pepper, diced
1 garlic clove, crushed and finely chopped
½ onion, diced
2 spring onions, white and some green parts sliced
1 tbsp Crushed Toasted Sesame Seeds (see page 22)
2 tsp sesame oil
1 tbsp soy sauce
175g/6oz mung beansprouts
vegetable oil for frying
Seasoned Dipping Sauce (see page 75) to serve

❖ Rub the beans, without draining them, between your palms to detach the skin. Pour off the water, which will take a lot of the skins with it. Cover the beans again and repeat the process until all the skins have been removed. Put the beans into a blender or food processor.

❖ Drain the rice and add to the blender or food processor with 4 tablespoons water. Mix to a paste then, with the motor running, slowly pour in 115ml/4fl oz water. Pour into a bowl and stir in the red pepper, garlic, onion, spring onions, sesame seeds, sesame oil and soy sauce.

❖ Add the mung beansprouts to a saucepan of boiling water. Cover and quickly return to the boil. Boil for 2 minutes then drain and squeeze out as much water as possible. Separate the beansprouts and stir into the batter.

❖ Heat a little oil in frying-pan, preferably non-stick. Stir the batter and add a ladleful to the pan, spreading it out evenly with the back of the ladle. Trickle 1 teaspoon vegetable oil over the top of the pancake, cover the pan and cook the pancake for 2½–3 minutes.

❖ Turn the pancake over and cook, uncovered, for a further 2½–3 minutes.

❖ Slide the pancake on to a warmed plate and cook the remaining batter in the same way.

SPRING ONION PANCAKES

Pajon I

These delicious pancakes are one of Korea's national dishes (rather confusingly they are known as "Korean pizzas"; they bear only a tenuous resemblance to Italian pizzas). They are served straight from the sizzling pan, cut into squares so they can be picked up easily with chopsticks.

SERVES 3-4

75g/3oz plain flour
75g/3oz rice flour
salt
1 large egg, beaten
1 tsp sesame oil
3 tbsp vegetable oil
6 spring onions, quartered lengthways, each length cut into 7.5cm/3in long strips
Vinegar Dipping Sauce (see page 32) to serve

◄ *Spring Onion Pancakes (right) and Spring Onion and Prawn Pancakes*

❖ Stir together the flours and salt. Stir in the egg, then slowly pour in 225ml/8fl oz water, stirring, to make a smooth batter. Stir in the sesame oil. Leave for 30 minutes.

❖ Heat 1 tbsp vegetable oil in a 20cm/8in non-stick frying-pan over a medium-low heat. Sprinkle one third of the spring onions evenly over the bottom then pour over one third of the batter. Cover and cook for 5–6 minutes. Turn the pancake, cover again and cook for a further 3 minutes. Remove the lid and cook for another 2 minutes. Transfer to a warm plate and repeat.

❖ Cut the pancakes into 5cm/2in squares and serve hot with the Vinegar Dipping Sauce.

SPRING ONION AND PRAWN PANCAKES

Pajon 2

This is a more elaborate version of the previous recipe. Break and lightly beat the eggs as you need them.

SERVES 4-6

115g/4oz plain flour
115g/4oz rice flour
salt and freshly ground black pepper
about 5 eggs
2 tsp sesame oil
dash of soy sauce
vegetable oil for frying
10 large spring onions, white and some green parts split lengthways and cut into strips
1 red pepper, cut into strips
1 courgette, cut into strips
115g/4oz cooked, peeled prawns
Ginger Dipping Sauce (see page 35) to serve

❖ Season the flours then stir in two of the eggs the sesame oil and soy sauce. Slowly pour in about 150ml/5fl oz water, stirring, to make a medium-thick batter. Leave for 30 minutes.

❖ Heat a very fine layer of vegetable oil in a large frying-pan, preferably non-stick. Pour in one third of the batter. Scatter over one third of the spring onions, pepper, courgette and prawns. Cook over a medium-hot heat for 5–7 minutes until set and browned underneath. Carefully turn over the pancake and cook for a further 5–7 minutes.

❖ Cook the remaining batter, vegetables, prawns and eggs in the same way. Serve, cut into squares, with Ginger Dipping Sauce.

NINE-SECTION APPETIZER

Kujolpan

Traditionally, small pancakes are served in a pile surrounded by a circle of eight fillings, all in their own lacquered dish. Each person takes a pancake and fills it with whichever filling they like, then rolls it up with their fingers. Kijolpan is great for relaxed leisurely eating with friends whether you serve it as a first course or a snack. The fillings should all look different and provide a variety of tastes and textures. This recipe may look complicated but each of the fillings is very quick and easy to prepare. A *kimchi* (see pages 40–64) could be used in place of one of the fillings.

SERVES 4-6

115g/4oz plain flour
salt and freshly ground black pepper
vegetable oil for frying

CUCUMBER FILLING

salt
½ cucumber, sliced into thin strips
2 tsp sesame oil

MUSHROOM FILLING

6 shiitake mushrooms, sliced
2–3 tsp sesame oil
1 tsp soy sauce
freshly ground black pepper

MEAT FILLING

115g/4oz sirloin or rump steak, cut into very fine strips
1 small garlic clove, crushed and finely chopped
1 spring onion, white part and a little green part, finely chopped
1 tbsp soy sauce
1 tsp Crushed Toasted Sesame Seeds (see page 22)
freshly ground black pepper
1½–2 tsp sesame oil

BAMBOO SHOOT FILLING

115g/4oz bamboo shoots, cut into fine strips
1cm/½in piece of fresh ginger, cut into very fine strips
1½ tsp soy sauce
1 tsp sesame oil

EGG FILLING

2 eggs,
salt and freshly ground black pepper
vegetable oil for frying

CARROT FILLING

- **I carrot, cut into very fine strips**
- **I tsp rice vinegar**
- **I tsp sugar**

PRAWN FILLING

- **115g/4oz peeled cooked prawns, chopped**
- **1½ tsp rice vinegar**
- **pinch of Korean chilli pepper, or cayenne pepper mixed with paprika**
- **salt**

❖ To make the pancakes, sift the flour and seasoning into a bowl, then slowly pour in about 175–200ml/6–7fl oz water to make a smooth batter. Leave for 30 minutes.

❖ Heat a very shallow layer of oil in a frying-pan, add spoonfuls of the batter and spread out to form 7.5cm/3in diameter circles. Fry until lightly browned on both sides. Stack in piles in a small shallow round serving dish.

❖ To make the cucumber filling, put the cucumber in a colander, sprinkle with salt and leave for 30 minutes. Rinse well and squeeze out as much water as possible. Heat the sesame oil in a frying-pan and fry the cucumber for 2–3 minutes. Transfer to a small serving dish.

❖ To make the mushroom filling, heat the oil in a frying-pan, add the mushrooms and stir-fry for 3–4 minutes. Toss with the soy sauce and transfer to a small serving dish.

❖ To make the meat filling, mix the beef with the garlic, spring onion, soy sauce, sesame seeds and pepper. Heat the sesame oil in a frying-pan, add the beef mixture and stir-fry for 4–5 minutes. Transfer to a small serving dish.

❖ To make the bamboo shoot filling, mix the bamboo shoots with the ginger and soy sauce. Heat the sesame oil in a frying-pan and stir-fry the bamboo shoots for 2–3 minutes. Transfer to a small serving dish.

❖ To make the egg filling, lightly beat the yolks and the whites with the seasoning. Heat the oil in a frying-pan, fry the egg to make an "omelette" and cut into strips (see page 85). Transfer to a small serving dish.

❖ To make the carrot filling, mix all the ingredients together. Transfer to a small serving dish.

❖ To make the prawn filling, mix all the ingredients together. Transfer to a small serving dish.

❖ To assemble the appetizer, put the dish of pancakes in the centre and arrange the other dishes in a circle around it.

GRILLED PORK BELLY

Samgyopsalgui

Samgyopsalgui are rather like a Korean version of Spanish *tapas* because they are served to customers in city *suljip* (or drinking houses) in order to increase thirst and therefore drink sales. Plates of thinly sliced rolled belly of pork are given to customers who cook it themselves on table-top burners and then dip the crisp, slightly charred, morsels in a simple sesame oil and salt dip.

SERVES 6

450g/1lb belly of pork, thinly sliced
about 4 tbsp sesame oil
2 tsp sea salt

❖ Preheat the grill or barbecue, or use a table-top burner. Stir together the sesame oil and salt in a small serving bowl.

❖ Cook the pork slices until crisp and slightly charred. Drain quickly on paper towels and serve hot with the dip. Don't forget to offer plenty of paper napkins.

CRISP KELP

Tasima

Tasima is the Korean name for kelp, which is more widely known by the Japanese name of *konbu*, also spelled *kombu*. It is sold in thick slices and is available from ethnic and healthfood shops. When deep-fried like this so that it is crisp on the outside yet chewy to eat, it is a favourite "nibble" with drinks. Do not wash the *tasima* but wipe it just before frying.

SERVES 4

vegetable oil for deep-frying
2 tbsp sesame oil
about 75g/3oz *tasima*, cut into 4cm/1½in long strips
sugar for sprinkling (optional)

❖ Half fill a deep-fat fryer with vegetable oil and add the sesame oil. Heat it to 180°C/350°F. Add the *tasima* in batches if necessary, so the pan is not crowded, and fry for about 10 seconds until the surface blisters and crackles; do not allow it to burn. Transfer to paper towels to drain. Serve hot, sprinkled with a little sugar, if liked.

KOREAN STEAK TARTARE

Yukhoe

Yukhoe is similar to steak tartare but there are important differences – whereas fillet steak is used for steak tartare, rump steak is considered better for Yukhoe. Yukhoe is also more highly seasoned.

SERVES 4

450g/1lb piece of rump steak, frozen for 1 hour
1 tbsp rice wine or dry sherry
3 tbsp soy sauce
1 tbsp sesame oil
1 tbsp Crushed Toasted Sesame Seeds (see page 22)
1 tbsp sugar
2½ garlic cloves, crushed and finely chopped
1cm/½in piece of fresh ginger, finely chopped
spring onions, white and green part thinly sliced on the diagonal
freshly ground black pepper
toasted sesame seeds to garnish

❖ Using a very sharp knife, cut the beef across the grain into wafer-thin slices. Pile the slices into stacks and cut across into very fine matchsticks. Put into a large bowl.

❖ Add the rice wine or dry sherry, soy sauce, sesame oil and sesame seeds, sugar, garlic, ginger and plenty of pepper. Mix gently but thoroughly – in Korea this would be done with the hands. Form into a loose ball, cover and chill for 1–2 hours.

❖ Using your hands, mound the beef on a cold serving plate and garnish with spring onions and toasted sesame seeds.

SESAME-GRILLED SEAWEED

Kimgui

Crisp, smoky, nutty-tasting, paper-thin sheets of grilled *kim* or laver (also known as *nori*) are an extremely moreish "nibble" to serve with drinks.

SERVES ABOUT 4

8–10 sheets *kim* (laver or *nori*)
sesame oil for brushing
salt
toasted sesame seeds to serve

❖ Brush both sides of each sheet of *kim* with sesame oil and sprinkle with salt.

❖ Hold each sheet in turn in tongs and pass backwards and forwards over a fairly low gas flame until crisp.

❖ Sprinkle the *kim* sheets with toasted sesame seeds. Leave people to break off pieces as they like, or cut the sheets into strips or squares.

EGG STRIP BUNDLES

Chon

Egg strips are tied in bundles with "strings" of blanched spring onion. In Korea the eggs are cooked in rectangular pans; as these are difficult to find here you can use an ordinary round crêpe or frying-pan and trim the curves of the "omelettes". Serve with whichever dipping sauce you like, or even a selection of them.

SERVES 4-6

5 eggs
salt and freshly ground black pepper
12 spring onions, trimmed
vegetable oil for frying
Dipping Sauce of choice (see vinegar page 32, sesame page 58, and ginger page 35) to serve

❖ Lightly beat the eggs with the seasoning.

❖ Heat a very fine layer of oil in a 15cm/6in frying-pan, preferably non-stick. Pour in half of the eggs, cover and cook over a low heat for 5–6 minutes until the bottom of the "omelette" is firm. Using a spatula, turn the "omelette" over and cook for a further 2–3 minutes until the second side is firm. Remove and allow to cool. Cook the remaining egg in the same way.

❖ Lower the spring onions, bulbs first into a saucepan of boiling water, easing in the green parts as they soften. Cover and quickly return to the boil. Boil for 2 minutes then drain and rinse under running cold water. Dry on paper towels. Split each spring onion lengthways into two or more strands by cutting through the bulb then tearing upwards.

❖ Trim the curves of the "omelettes" then cut the "omelettes" into strips about 6cm/2½in long by 5mm/¼in wide.

❖ Make bundles of eight to ten egg strips each. Wrap a strip of spring onion around the centre of each bundle and tuck the end of the spring onion under the binding. Arrange the bundles on a serving plate and serve with a dipping sauce.

STUFFED CHILLIES

Kochujon

Touching chillies can make your hands, particularly any cuts or bruises, sting so it is a good idea to wear fine rubber gloves when preparing this dish. Serve Kochujon as a first course.

SERVES 4

225g/8oz lean pork, freshly minced
1 garlic clove, finely chopped
1cm/½in piece of fresh ginger, finely chopped
4 spring onions, finely chopped
2 tsp Crushed Toasted Sesame Seeds (see page 22)
2–3 tsp soy sauce
16–20 large fresh red chillies
seasoned plain flour for coating
1 large egg, beaten
vegetable oil for frying
Vinegar Dipping Sauce (see below) to serve

❖ Mix the pork, garlic, ginger, spring onions, sesame seeds and soy sauce together very well.

❖ Cut the chillies in half lengthways and remove the seeds. Break off small pieces of the meat mixture to fill the chillies, form into torpedo shapes and use to stuff the chillies, packing the meat stuffing in firmly.

❖ Roll the stuffed chillies in seasoned flour to give an even coating, then dip in beaten egg.

❖ Heat a 1cm/½in layer of oil in a frying-pan. Add the chillies in batches and fry for 4–5 minutes a side until golden brown and cooked through. Remove from the oil with a slotted spoon and drain on paper towels. Serve hot with Vinegar Dipping Sauce.

VINEGAR DIPPING SAUCE

Chojang I

This can serve as a basic Korean dipping sauce.

MAKES 10 TBSP

7 tbsp soy sauce
2 tbsp rice vinegar
1cm/½in piece of fresh ginger, grated
2 tsp Crushed Toasted Sesame Seeds
about ½ tsp Korean chilli powder
pinch of sugar

❖ Combine the soy sauce and vinegar in a small bowl, and add remaining ingredients. If you do not have the chilli powder, use cayenne pepper mixed with paprika.

Stuffed Chillies ▶

KOREAN CRAB CAKES

Kejon

Although not quite authentic, I like to serve Kejon with a crisp green salad.

SERVES 4

350g/12oz floury potatoes, unpeeled
1½ garlic cloves, crushed and finely chopped
1 fresh red chilli, seeded and finely chopped
2.5cm/1in piece of fresh ginger, grated
3 spring onions, finely chopped
225g/8oz white and brown crabmeat
finely grated rind of ½ lime
2 tbsp chopped fresh coriander
salt and freshly ground black pepper
1½ tbsp sesame seeds
50g/2oz fresh breadcrumbs, for coating
flour for coating
flour for coating
1 egg, beaten
vegetable oil for deep-frying
Ginger Dipping Sauce (see below) to serve

◀ *Korean Crab Cakes*

❖ Boil the potatoes in their skins until tender. Drain and leave until cool enough to handle. Peel the potatoes and mash the flesh.

❖ Mix the mashed potato with the garlic, chilli, ginger, spring onions, crabmeat, lime zest, coriander and salt and pepper. Form into eight round cakes about the size of golf balls. Chill for 30 minutes.

❖ Stir the sesame seeds into the breadcrumbs. Coat the crab cakes in the flour then the egg and finally coat in the breadcrumbs, pressing in the crumbs firmly.

❖ Half fill a deep-fat fryer with vegetable oil and heat to about 170°C/325°F. Fry the crab cakes in batches for about 8 minutes until golden. Transfer to paper towels to drain while frying the remaining crab cakes. Serve hot with Ginger Dipping Sauce.

GINGER DIPPING SAUCE

Chojang 2

There are no chillies in this sauce but ginger provides some "hotness". Also the predominance of soy sauce and rice vinegar are reversed.

MAKES ABOUT 10 TBSP

6 tbsp rice vinegar
2.5cm/1in piece of fresh ginger, grated
2 spring onions, white part only, finely chopped
2 tbsp dark soy sauce
2 tsp sugar

❖ Pour the vinegar into a small bowl. Add the remaining ingredients and mix together well.

OYSTER FRITTERS

Kulwigim

Use Pacific oysters for these fritters – not only are they the authentic ones, but they are cheaper than European flat oysters, also known in Britain as "native" oysters. Save the liquid that is in the oyster shells to strain into the batter; reduce the water by the amount of oyster liquid added and omit the salt from the recipe if you do this.

Add some sesame seeds to the batter if liked, for an extra nutty, crunchy texture.

SERVES 4-6

115g/4oz plain flour
2 tsp baking powder
very small pinch of Korean chilli powder, or cayenne pepper mixed with paprika
salt
1 egg, beaten
about 24 oysters, opened
vegetable oil for deep-frying
Sesame or Vinegar Dipping Sauce (see pages 58 and 32) to serve

❖ Sift the flour, baking powder, Korean chilli powder, or cayenne pepper and paprika, and salt into a bowl. Slowly pour in 150ml/5 fl oz water, stirring, to make a smooth batter. Leave for 30 minutes.

❖ Half fill a deep-fat fryer with vegetable oil and heat to about 180°C/350°F. Dip the oysters in the batter then fry for about 2 minutes until the batter is crisp and golden; take care not to overcook the oysters as they will become tough.

❖ Drain the oysters on paper towels and serve hot with Sesame or Vinegar Dipping Sauce.

ABOVE *Fishing is prevalent in Korea, providing a wealth of fish, shellfish and sea vegetables.*

CRISPY ANCHOVIES

Marunmyolchi

The dried anchovies for this dish are about the size of whitebait and are deep-fried in the same way. They can be found in most Japanese supermarkets. If the anchovies are very salted, rub or rinse off excess salt before frying. Deep-fried anchovies mixed with a sweet/hot sauce which contrast with their saltiness, are extremely moreish.

SERVES 4

1 garlic clove, finely chopped
1 small onion, chopped
1 fresh red chilli, seeded
¾ tsp salt
1½ tsp sugar
2 tbsp vegetable oil, plus extra for deep-frying
about 115g/4oz dried anchovies, heads removed if liked, rinsed if necessary
fresh coriander leaves for garnish

❖ Grind the garlic, onion and chilli to a paste with the salt. Mix in the sugar. Set aside.

❖ Heat the 2 tablespoons vegetable oil in a frying-pan, add the onion paste and cook, stirring occasionally, for 3–4 minutes. Meanwhile, half fill a deep-fat fryer with vegetable oil and heat to 180°C/350°F. Add the anchovies so the pan is not crowded (in batches if necessary) and fry for 20–30 seconds until very crisp and lightly coloured.

❖ Transfer the anchovies to paper towels to drain then tip into the frying-pan and heat through, shaking the pan. Pour into a serving bowl and garnish with coriander leaves.

STEAMED PORK AND PRAWN CUSTARD

Altchim

For this pork- and prawn-packed custard you will need a shallow flameproof dish that will fit inside a steaming basket. Alternatively, the mixture may be steamed in four individual dishes for 12–15 minutes.

SERVES 4

115g/4oz lean minced pork
1 tbsp soy sauce
1 tsp sesame oil
1 garlic clove, crushed and finely chopped
5mm/¼in piece of fresh ginger, grated
4 eggs
1 tsp toasted sesame seeds
50g/2oz cooked peeled prawns
2 spring onions, white part and a little green part finely chopped
freshly ground black pepper

❖ Mix together the pork, soy sauce, sesame oil, garlic and ginger. Add to a shallow flameproof dish and fry, stirring to break up the pork, until the pork has changed colour.

❖ Beat the eggs with a little water.

❖ Remove the dish from the heat and stir in the eggs, sesame seeds, prawns, spring onions and pepper. Cover with greaseproof paper and place in a steaming basket. Put the steaming basket over a saucepan of boiling water and steam for 17–20 minutes until the custard is just set in the centre.

Salads, Vegetables and Pickled Vegetables

Korean salads, often made from lightly steamed or fried vegetables, are simply and lightly dressed with soy sauce, sesame oil and rice vinegar, and usually flavoured with the characteristic flavourings – garlic, ginger, spring onions and chilli.

A selection of salads and vegetables are served as part of the *panchan* (side dishes) that accompany Korean meals. Pickled vegetables, *kimchis* in particular, are a Korean passion and no cook worth their salt would serve a proper meal without at least one *kimchi*.

SPINACH SALAD

Shigumchinamul

This salad is equally good served warm or chilled.

SERVES 4

450g/1lb young fresh spinach leaves
1 garlic clove, crushed and finely chopped
1 tbsp sesame oil
2 tbsp soy sauce
2 tsp sesame seeds
freshly ground black pepper

❖ Add the spinach to a large saucepan of boiling water. Cover and quickly return to the boil. Boil for 1 minute then tip the spinach into a colander and refresh under running cold water. Drain, then dry on paper towels.

❖ Coarsely shred the spinach, then toss with the remaining ingredients. Serve warm, or leave until cold then cover and chill. Toss again before serving.

BEANSPROUT SALAD

Kongnamul

This is a much loved, crunchy, nutritious salad or side dish. In restaurants it may be served with your pre-prandial drinks so you have something to nibble while you are waiting for your meal to arrive.

SERVES 4-6

675g/1½lb soy beansprouts or mung beansprouts
2 garlic cloves, very finely chopped
5 spring onions, white and green parts thinly sliced into rings
1 fresh hot red chilli, seeded and thinly sliced into rings
1 tbsp Crushed Toasted Sesame Seeds (see page 22)
salt

❖ Remove the roots from the beansprouts. Add the beansprouts to a pan of boiling water. Return to the boil, then tip into a colander and rinse under running cold water. Squeeze as much water as possible from the beansprouts.

❖ Toss the beansprouts with the remaining ingredients. Serve at room temperature or slightly chilled.

Beansprout Salad (left) and Spinach Salad ▶

WHITE RADISH PICKLE

Kakdooki

Some people find that chillies and chilli powder irritate their skin; if this happens to you, wear fine rubber gloves when rubbing the chilli powder into the radish.

FILLS A 900ML/1½PT JAR

2 tbsp Korean chilli powder or cayenne pepper mixed with paprika
800g/1¾lb white radish, cut into 2.5cm/1in cubes
4 spring onions, white and green parts thinly sliced
2.5cm/1in piece of fresh ginger, finely chopped
1 small garlic clove, finely chopped
2 tsp sugar
4 tsp salt

❖ Rub the chilli powder or cayenne and paprika into the white radish, put in a bowl and leave for 30 minutes.

❖ Mix the remaining ingredients with the white radish and cover with a sheet of cling film. Put a plate that just fits inside the bowl, on top of the cling film, and put a heavy weight on top. Leave for about 48 hours until the liquid rises above the white radish.

❖ Remove the weight and leave the pickle for 3–7 days, depending on temperature, until it turns sour.

❖ Transfer the pickle to a dry, clean 900ml/1½pt jar, cover with a vinegar-proof lid and keep in a cold, dark place. It will keep for up to a year in these conditions.

ABOVE *Local food markets with hustle and bustle and a warm atmosphere are a common sight throughout Korea.*

WHITE RADISH SALAD

Muusaengchae I

In Korea, they use long, pointed white radishes that are known in the West by the Japanese name of *daikon* or the Indian name of *mooli*. They are available in some greengrocers as well as ethnic shops.

SERVES 3-4

1 white radish, coarsely grated or cut lengthways into fine strips
salt
½–1 tsp Korean chilli powder, or cayenne pepper mixed with paprika
2 tsp sugar
1 tbsp sesame oil
4 tbsp rice vinegar
1cm/½in piece of fresh ginger, finely chopped
sesame seeds for garnish

❖ Put the white radish into a colander, mix with salt and leave for 10–15 minutes.

❖ Rinse the radish well, drain then dry thoroughly on paper towels.

❖ Toss the radish with the remaining ingredients, except the sesame seeds. Cover and chill. Garnish with sesame seeds to serve.

CUCUMBER SALAD

Oinamul

Mixing the cucumber with salt and leaving it for 1 hour draws out moisture so preventing the sauce from being watery.

SERVES 2-4

1 long cucumber, very thinly sliced
salt
pinch of Korean chilli powder, or cayenne pepper mixed with paprika
1 tbsp sugar
2 tbsp rice vinegar
sesame oil for sprinkling

❖ Put the cucumber slices in a bowl, toss with salt then add cold water to cover. Leave for 1 hour. Drain the cucumber. If the cucumber tastes very salty rinse it under running cold water then dry very well on paper towels. Put the cucumber into a bowl.

❖ Mix the Korean chilli powder, or cayenne pepper and paprika, with the sugar and vinegar and pour over the cucumber. Sprinkle with sesame oil and toss to mix. Cover and chill. Toss again before serving.

AUBERGINE SALAD WITH SESAME SEEDS

Khajinamul

Khajinamul doubles as a salad and a first course; it is usually served at the beginning of a meal then left on the table until the end.

SERVES 4-6

550g/1 ¼lb oriental aubergines, or small, slim aubergines
1 spring onion, white and green part sliced into rings
1 tbsp sugar
1 tbsp sesame oil
3 tbsp Japanese soy sauce
2 garlic cloves, finely chopped
2 tbsp rice vinegar
2 tbsp Crushed Toasted Sesame Seeds (see page 22)
salt

❖ If using oriental aubergines, cut them lengthways into quarters then slice across the middle of each piece. If using ordinary aubergines, cut them into long pieces about 2.5cm/1in thick and 2.5cm/1in wide.

❖ Steam the pieces of aubergine in a covered container until tender and soft.

❖ Meanwhile, mix together the remaining ingredients.

❖ Leave the aubergines until cool enough to handle then tear into long, thin strips. Put into a bowl, pour over the dressing mixture and stir together. Serve at room temperature, or chill before serving.

LOTUS ROOT SALAD

Namul

Lotus roots have a firm, crunchy texture, a taste similar to artichoke hearts and the slices display an attractive flower-like pattern.

SERVES 2-4

115g/4oz young lotus roots, thinly sliced
2 tbsp soy sauce
1 tbsp rice vinegar
2 tsp sesame oil
2 tsp toasted sesame seeds
1 tsp sugar

❖ Arrange the lotus roots in a steaming basket, cover and put over a saucepan of boiling water. Steam for about 1 hour – the time will depend on the age and therefore toughness of the roots.

❖ Transfer the lotus roots to a bowl, add the remaining ingredients and stir together. Serve warm or chilled.

CARROT AND WHITE RADISH SALAD

Mou Sangchae

Both the colours and flavours of white radish and carrot compliment each other in this attractive salad.

SERVES 4

1 carrot, thinly sliced on the diagonal
225g/8oz white radish, cut into fine strips
salt
1 tbsp sesame oil
1 tsp soy sauce
1 tsp sugar
very small pinch of Korean chilli powder, or cayenne pepper mixed with paprika

❖ Cut the carrot slices into very fine strips and put into a bowl with the white radish strips. Sprinkle lightly with salt, toss together well then leave for 1 hour. Drain then rinse and drain thoroughly, pressing out as much liquid as possible. Dry on paper towels.

❖ Mix the vegetables with the remaining ingredients and serve.

◄ *Carrot and White Radish Salad (above) and Lotus Root Salad*

MUSHROOMS BAKED IN FOIL

Posot

Cooking mushrooms in foil so the aroma, flavour and juices are trapped inside is a speciality of many of Korea's older, traditional restaurants. The unseasoned mushrooms are either eaten plain, with a dipping sauce or as a contrast to hot and garlicky dishes.

SERVES 2-4

175g/6oz large white mushrooms, caps and stalks cut into 5mm/¼in slices
Vinegar Dipping Sauce (see page 32) (optional)

❖ Cut a large piece of foil – about 50 x 30cm/ 20 x 12in. Put the mushrooms in the centre of the foil. Fold over the long sides of the foil then the short sides to make a neat, secure parcel.

❖ Pre-heat a barbecue or grill. Cook the mushroom parcels about 10cm/4in from the heat for 5–7 minutes.

❖ Serve the mushrooms straightaway, accompanied by a dipping sauce if liked.

COOKED WATERCRESS SALAD

Minarinamul

Steaming the watercress rather than boiling it keeps it drier and saves having to strain it.

SERVES 4

2 large bunches watercress
3 tbsp soy sauce
1 tbsp sesame oil
2 tsp toasted sesame seeds
salt and freshly ground black pepper

❖ Cut off and discard the coarse parts of the watercress stalks then spread it out in a shallow layer in a steaming basket; you may have to cook the watercress in two batches if the steaming basket is not very large. Cover the basket and put over a saucepan of boiling water. Steam for 1–2 minutes. Remove the watercress from the steaming basket and coarsely chop it.

❖ Toss the watercress with the soy sauce, sesame oil and seeds, salt and pepper. Leave until cold, then cover and chill. Toss again before serving.

MUSHROOMS WITH CHICKEN AND VEGETABLES

Posotbokkum

Mushrooms of many different types are very popular in Korea. The most widely available of these in the West are both fresh and dried shiitake (when dried they are more commonly known as dried Chinese black mushrooms), dried wood ear (also known as cloud ear and tree ear), which have little flavour but a pleasing texture and attractive appearance, and stone mushrooms.

SERVES 3-4

175g/6oz chicken breast, cut into strips
3 garlic cloves, crushed and finely chopped
4 tbsp soy sauce
2 tsp sesame oil
freshly ground black pepper
vegetable oil for frying
450g/1lb shitake or oyster mushrooms, thinly sliced
1 red pepper, cut into thin strips
1 courgette, thinly sliced diagonally
4 spring onions, white and some green parts thinly sliced diagonally
fresh coriander leaves for garnish

❖ Mix the chicken with the garlic, soy sauce, sesame oil and plenty of black pepper. Leave for 30 minutes.

❖ Heat a little vegetable oil in a large frying-pan. Lift the chicken from the marinade (reserve the marinade) and stir-fry for 2 minutes or so.

❖ Stir in all the vegetables and cook, stirring, for about 5 minutes until the vegetables are tender but still crisp. Stir in the reserved marinade about 1 minute before the end of cooking. Serve garnished with coriander leaves.

ABOVE *Mount Chirisan in Spring. A National Park, famous for outstanding beauty and superb hiking.*

STIR-FRY PORK AND VEGETABLE SALAD

Twaepyon

The vegetables can be altered according to taste or availability.

SERVES 4

vegetable oil for frying
115/4oz piece of pork loin, cut into fine strips
1 small turnip, cut into 5cm/2in long strips
1 small carrot, cut into 5cm/2in long strips
1 small onion, cut into 5cm/2in long strips
2–3 celery stalks, cut into 5cm/2in long strips
50g/2oz mushroom caps, cut into 5cm/2in long strips
1 small garlic clove, crushed and finely chopped
1 tsp grated fresh root ginger
2 spring onions, white and some green parts finely chopped
3 tbsp soy sauce
1½ tsp sesame oil
1 tbsp sugar
1 tsp rice vinegar
freshly ground black pepper
sesame seeds for garnish

❖ Heat about 2 tablespoons of oil in a frying-pan, add the pork and stir-fry for 3–4 minutes until cooked through. Using a slotted spoon, remove it to a bowl.

❖ Add the turnip and carrot strips to the pan and fry for 5–7 minutes until just beginning to soften.

❖ Add the onion and celery to a saucepan of boiling water and simmer for 2–3 minutes. Drain and refresh under running cold water. Add to the pork with the mushrooms, garlic, ginger and spring onions.

❖ Using a slotted spoon transfer the turnips and carrots to kitchen paper to drain.

❖ Whisk together the soy sauce, sesame oil, sugar and rice vinegar. Add the turnips and carrots to the pork, pour over the dressing and toss. Leave until cold. Serve sprinkled with sesame seeds.

SPICED WHITE RADISH SALAD

Muusaengchae 2

White radishes have a milder flavour than Western red radishes so respond well to being mixed with typical Korean flavourings.

SERVES 4

1 large white radish, sliced
salt
1 tbsp soy sauce
2 tsp rice vinegar
1cm/½in piece of fresh ginger, finely chopped
1 tsp sugar
2 tsp Crushed Toasted Sesame Seeds (see page 22)
1½ tsp *kochujang* (see page 69) or chilli bean paste
1 garlic clove, finely chopped
1 spring onion, white and green part thinly sliced diagonally

❖ Put the white radish into a colander, mix with salt and leave for 10–15 minutes.

❖ Rinse the radish well, drain then dry thoroughly on paper towels.

❖ Mix together the remaining ingredients, except the spring onions, and toss with the white radish. Scatter over the spring onions, cover and chill. Toss lightly before serving.

◄ *Soy-Glazed Pumpkin*

SOY-GLAZED PUMPKIN

Yachaejorim

The mixture of pumpkin with ginger and soy sauce gives attractive colour, taste and texture combinations.

SERVES 4

225g/8oz pumpkin, cut into 2.5cm/1in cubes
115g/4oz sugar
5cm/2in piece of fresh ginger, grated
6 tbsp soy sauce
freshly ground black pepper
toasted sesame seeds and garlic chives for garnish

❖ Cook the pumpkin in boiling water for 2 minutes. Drain well then put into a frying-pan. Add 6 tablespoons of water, the sugar, ginger, soy sauce and pepper. Heat gently, stirring carefully, until the sugar dissolves. Then partially cover and simmer gently for about 15 minutes, stirring occasionally, until the pumpkin is tender and glazed with soy syrup.

❖ Garnish with sesame seeds and garlic chives.

COURGETTES WITH BEEF

Hobakmuchim

Hobakmuchim is a simple but very tasty dish that can be served in traditional Korean manner with *kimchis*, rice, salads and vegetables, or Western-style with a green vegetable or salad.

SERVES 2-4

4 small courgettes, cut diagonally into 5mm/¼in slices
salt
115g/4oz lean beef, freshly minced
2 tbsp vegetable oil
2 spring onions, white and green parts very thinly sliced
1 tbsp sugar
1 tbsp soy sauce
½–1 tsp chilli powder
toasted sesame seeds for garnish

MARINADE

1 spring onion, white and green part very thinly sliced
2 garlic cloves, crushed and finely chopped
1½ tbsp soy sauce
1 tbsp sesame oil
2.5cm/1in piece of fresh ginger, finely chopped
1 tbsp toasted sesame seeds
freshly ground black pepper

❖ Put the courgettes in a colander, sprinkle generously with salt, toss together and leave for 30 minutes. Meanwhile mix all the marinade ingredients together, add the minced beef and leave for 30 minutes.

❖ Rinse the courgettes well and dry thoroughly with paper towels. Heat the vegetable oil in a large frying-pan over a fairly high heat, add the beef and marinade and fry, stirring to break up the lumps, for about 1 minute or until the beef changes colour.

❖ Gently stir in the courgettes then add the remaining ingredients, except the sesame seeds. Cook for 2 minutes, stirring gently. Lower the heat and continue to stir for a further minute until the courgettes are tender but still retain some bite.

❖ Serve sprinkled with toasted sesame seeds.

FRIED COURGETTES WITH SESAME SEEDS

Hobakjon

A coating of sesame seeds gives courgettes an interesting nutty flavour and crunchy/crisp texture.

SERVES 4

550g/1 ¼lb small courgettes, cut diagonally into 5mm/¼in thick slices
salt
seasoned plain flour for coating
1 large egg, beaten
sesame seeds for coating
vegetable oil for frying
Sesame Dipping Sauce (see page 58) or Vinegar Dipping Sauce (see page 32) to serve

(clockwise from left) Fried Courgettes with Sesame Seeds, Carrot Fritters, and Deep-Fried Aubergines (p58) ▶

❖ Put the courgettes into a colander, toss generously with salt and leave for 30 minutes.

❖ Rinse the courgettes well and dry thoroughly with paper towels. Toss the courgettes in seasoned plain flour to coat evenly, then dip in beaten egg. Then coat in sesame seeds.

❖ Heat a thin layer of oil in a wide frying-pan, add the courgette slices in a single layer and fry for 3–4 minutes a side until golden on the outside but still crisp on the inside.

❖ Using a slotted spoon, transfer to paper towels to drain. Serve hot with Sesame or Vinegar Dipping Sauce.

CARROT FRITTERS

Hobak

Any of the dipping sauces in this book can be served to accompany these carrot slices.

SERVES 2-4

2 carrots, thinly sliced diagonally
4 tbsp plain flour
1 large egg, beaten
vegetable oil for frying
Sesame Dipping Sauce (see page 58)

❖ Coat the carrot slices lightly and evenly in the flour then dip in beaten egg.

❖ Heat a 5mm/¼in layer of oil in a frying-pan, add the carrot slices and fry in a single layer until golden brown on both sides. Using a slotted spoon, transfer the carrot slices to paper towels to drain. Serve hot with a dipping sauce.

DEEP-FRIED AUBERGINES

Kajijon

Jon is the name given to ingredients that are coated in flour then dipped in egg and fried. These aubergine *jon* can be served as a first course, or to eat with drinks; in which case, supply cocktail sticks for spearing the aubergine slices.

SERVES 4

2 aubergines, thinly sliced on the diagonal
salt
plain flour for coating
Korean chilli powder, or cayenne pepper mixed with paprika
1–1½ tbsp chopped fresh coriander
1 large egg, beaten
oil for deep-frying
Sesame Dipping Sauce (see below) to serve

❖ Put the aubergine slices into a colander, toss with salt and leave for 30 minutes. Rinse the aubergine slices, drain and dry thoroughly on paper towels.

❖ Season some plain flour with salt and chilli powder, or cayenne and paprika, to taste and add the coriander. Toss the aubergine slices in the flour to coat evenly then dip in the beaten egg. Allow excess egg to drain off.

❖ Heat a deep-fat fryer half-filled with oil to 180°C/350°F. Add the aubergine slices in batches so the pan is not crowded and fry until golden brown. Drain on paper towels. Serve hot with Sesame Dipping Sauce.

SESAME DIPPING SAUCE

Chojang 3

Sesame oil and toasted sesame seeds make a more richly flavoured dipping sauce.

MAKES 6 TBSP

3 tbsp soy sauce
1 tsp sesame oil
1½ tbsp rice vinegar
1 tsp toasted sesame seeds
pinch of sugar
1 small spring onion, finely chopped

❖ Combine the soy sauce, sesame oil and rice vinegar in a small bowl. Add the remaining ingredients and mix well.

STUFFED CUCUMBER PICKLE

Oisobagi

Use a potato peeler or the slicing disc of a food processor to slice the white radish. To serve, slice through the cucumbers completely and arrange on a plate.

FILLS ABOUT 1.5 LITRES/2½PT JAR

675g/1½lb pickling cucumbers
salt
2.5cm/1in piece of fresh ginger, cut into paper thin slices
350g/12oz white radish, very thinly sliced
2 tbsp very finely chopped garlic
6 spring onions, white and some green parts very thinly sliced
2½ tsp Korean chilli powder, or cayenne pepper mixed with paprika
1½ tsp sugar

❖ Cut the cucumbers crossways, slightly diagonally, at 1cm/½in intervals but not going quite all the way through – the slices should remain attached at the bottom.

❖ Pour 1 litre/1¾pt water into a bowl and stir in 4 tablespoons of salt until dissolved. Add the cucumbers and weight down with a plate to keep them submerged. Leave for 3–4 hours.

❖ Just before the cucumbers are ready, stack the ginger slices and cut into very thin strips. Stack the white radish slices and cut across into very, very fine strips. If the strips are longer than 2.5cm/1in, cut them in half. Mix with the ginger, garlic, spring onions, sugar, chilli powder, or cayenne and paprika, and 2 teaspoons of salt.

❖ Lift the cucumbers from the liquid; reserve the liquid. Dry the cucumbers with paper towels. Fill the gaps between the cucumber slices with as much of the white radish stuffing as they will hold easily. Put into a bowl, add any remaining white radish stuffing and liquid from it, cover and leave for 8 hours.

❖ Carefully pack the cucumbers fairly tightly into a clean, dry 1.5 litre/2½pt jar. Push any loose stuffing between the cucumbers and pour in all the juices from the bowl. Push the cucumbers down; if the liquid does not cover them by 1cm/½in, add some of the reserved cucumber soaking water.

❖ Cover loosely and leave for 3–6 days until the pickle has soured to your taste. Seal tightly and keep until required. It will keep for up to a year.

SPICED TURNIP PICKLE

Sunmukimchi

Turnip is a very popular root vegetable in Korea, used in many daily recipes as well as in pickles.

FILLS A 350ML/12FL OZ JAR

2 turnips, each weighing about 150g/5oz, peeled, halved lengthways and thinly sliced
1½ tsp salt
3 garlic cloves, finely chopped
1 spring onion, white and green part finely chopped
1 dried red chilli, seeded and coarsely crushed

❖ Rub 1 teaspoon of the salt into the turnip slices then put into a bowl and leave for 3 hours, stirring the slices every 30 minutes.

❖ Drain the turnips and rinse under running cold water. Drain again then mix with the remaining ingredients.

❖ Pack into a clean, dry jar then cover with cold water. Put a saucer on the jar and leave for 6–8 days until the pickle turns sour.

❖ Cover the jar with a vinegar-proof lid and store in a cool, dry place for up to a year.

SPICED SWEET POTATO SLICES

Kogumajon

Traditionally these potato slices are served with a dipping sauce but they can also be served as a vegetable accompaniment.

SERVES 4

2 sweet potatoes, cut diagonally into 5mm/¼in thick slices
salt
plain flour for coating
chilli powder
1 large egg, beaten
vegetable oil for frying
Vinegar Dipping Sauce (see page 32) to serve

❖ Add the sweet potato slices to a saucepan of boiling salted water and cook for about 5 minutes. Drain well and dry on paper towels.

❖ Season the flour with chilli powder then coat the sweet potato slices evenly in the seasoned flour. Dip in beaten egg.

❖ Heat a thin layer of vegetable oil in a wide frying-pan, add a layer of sweet potato slices, and fry for about 4 minutes a side.

❖ Transfer to paper towels to drain. Serve hot with Vinegar Dipping Sauce.

CABBAGE PICKLE

Kimchi I

This is a standard cabbage *kimchi*. Some of the cabbage can be replaced by thinly sliced white radish, if liked.

FILLS A 2.25 LITRE/4PT JAR

900g/2lb Chinese cabbage
salt
6 spring onions, white and green parts thinly sliced
4 garlic cloves, crushed and finely chopped
2 tbsp finely chopped fresh ginger
1 tbsp Korean chilli powder, or cayenne pepper mixed with paprika
1 tsp sugar

❖ Quarter the Chinese cabbage lengthways, then cut each quarter widthwise into approximately 5cm/2in pieces.

❖ Pour 1.5 litres/2½pt water into a large bowl and stir in 3 tablespoons salt until dissolved. Add the cabbage and weight down with a plate to keep them submerged.

❖ Cover and leave for 12 hours, stirring the cabbage occasionally. Using a slotted spoon remove the cabbage from the bowl, and reserve the salted water.

❖ Mix the cabbage with the remaining ingredients and 1 teaspoon salt. Pack into a clean, dry 2.25 litre/4pt jar. Pour in enough of the reserved salted water to cover the cabbage; leave a space of 2.5cm/1in at the top of the jar. Cover the jar loosely with a non-metallic lid and leave for 3–6 days until the pickle has become sour enough for your taste. Cover tightly and keep in a cold, dark place. It will keep in these conditions for up to 1 year.

ABOVE *Many crafts and farming techniques are still based largely on tradition.*

PICKLED GARLIC

Manul

Green garlic is used in Korea for this recipe, but it works very well with ordinary garlic if the heads are made up of large, plump cloves. After pickling, the cut garlic heads are cut crossways to make attractive slices.

FILLS A 225ML/8FL OZ JAR

2 heads of garlic with plump cloves
115ml/4fl oz rice vinegar
115ml/4 fl oz soy sauce
2 tbsp sugar
1 tsp salt

❖ Put the garlic in a clean, dry 225ml/8fl oz jar. Bring the remaining ingredients to the boil in a small saucepan then simmer gently until reduced by half. Pour over the garlic, cover tightly and leave for 2 months. It will keep for up to a year in a cool, dry place.

INSTANT CUCUMBER PICKLE

Khachori

This is a very convenient version of *kimchi* as it can be eaten as soon as it has been chilled.

SERVES 6-8

450g/1lb cucumbers
2¼ tsp salt
1 garlic clove, crushed and finely chopped
3½in piece of white radish, cut into fine strips
2 spring onions, white and green parts thinly sliced
2.5cm/1in piece of fresh ginger, crushed to a pulp
1½ tsp Korean chilli powder, or cayenne pepper mixed with paprika
2 tsp Crushed Toasted Sesame Seeds (see page 22)
1 tbsp sesame oil

❖ Cut the cucumber into 5cm/2in lengths then cut each piece lengthways in half. Place each half skin-side up and slice across. Put the slices in a colander, toss with 2 teaspoons of the salt and leave for 3 hours.

❖ Drain the cucumber gently, squeezing out as much water as possible.

❖ Mix the cucumber with the remaining salt, garlic, white radish, spring onions, ginger and chilli powder, or cayenne and paprika. Cover and chill. Drain off the liquid from the vegetables then toss them with the sesame seeds and sesame oil. This will keep for a day or two in the fridge.

(clockwise from top right) Pickled Garlic, Instant Cucumber Pickle and Stuffed Cabbage Pickle (p64) ▶

STUFFED CABBAGE PICKLE

Kimchi 2

Salted fish, especially anchovies, are a popular addition to *kimchis*; the fish dissolve during the fermentation and storage, enriching the flavour of the *kimchi*, not giving it a fishy taste. For convenience, I have used fish sauce instead of salted anchovies.

FILLS A 225G/8FL OZ JAR

½ Chinese cabbage, about 225g/8oz
175g/6oz piece of white radish, halved crossways
4 spring onions, coarsely chopped
4 garlic cloves, crushed and finely chopped
2.5cm/1in piece of fresh ginger, crushed and finely chopped
1 tbsp Korean chilli powder, or cayenne pepper mixed with paprika
1 tsp sugar
2 tbsp fish sauce
100g/3½oz salt

❖ Pour 1 litre/1¾pt water into a large bowl and stir in all but ¼ tsp of the salt until dissolved. Add the cabbage and put a plate on top to keep it submerged. Leave for 8–10 hours.

❖ Cut the white radish into thin strips, then mix well with the remaining ingredients, including the remaining salt. Drain the cabbage well, then squeeze hard to remove as much water as possible.

❖ Place the cabbage cut-side up. Beginning with the outer leaves, pack the white radish mixture between each leaf.

❖ Fold the cabbage leaves and pack them into a clean, dry jar. Add any remaining white radish mixture. Cover loosely with vinegar-proof lids and leave for at least 3 days until sour enough for your taste. Push the cabbage down so it remains beneath the liquid that is produced. Cover tightly and keep in a cold place until required. It will keep for up to a year.

K
I
N
G

STIR-FRIED SQUID WITH CHILLIES AND VEGETABLES

Ojhingubokum

Both the hot, fermented bean paste, *kochujang*, and Korea's excellent coarsely pounded red chilli powder, are used in this spicy dish. The Korean chilli powder adds a characteristic bright, carmine pink colour. If necessary you can always use cayenne pepper mixed with paprika to obtain the same result. Chilli bean paste can also be substituted for the *kochuchang*.

SERVES 3-4

550g/1¼lb cleaned squid
3 tbsp vegetable oil
1 onion, thinly sliced
2 garlic cloves, crushed
1 carrot, thinly sliced lengthways
1 courgette, thinly sliced lengthways
2–3 long fresh red chillies, thinly sliced lengthways
2 long fresh green chillies, thinly sliced lengthways
1 tbsp *kochujang* (see page 69) or chilli bean paste
about ½tsp Korean chilli powder, or cayenne pepper mixed with paprika
1 tsp sugar
salt and freshly ground black pepper
2 spring onions, white and green parts sliced diagonally
2 tsp sesame oil
toasted sesame seeds to garnish

❖ Cut open each squid body so that it lies flat, then cut across into 6 x 1cm/2½ x ½in pieces. Cut the tentacles into 6cm/2½in lengths.

❖ Bring a large saucepan of water to the boil, add the squid in one go and remove from the heat. Stir immediately and continue to stir until the squid turns white, about 40 seconds. Drain well and discard the water.

❖ Heat the oil in a large frying-pan over a moderate heat. Add the onion, garlic and carrot. Stir for 30–40 seconds then add the courgette, chillies and 2 tsp *kochujang* or chilli bean paste, half the chilli powder or cayenne and paprika. Stir for 30 seconds. Stir in the squid, remaining *kochujang* and chilli powder or cayenne and paprika, sugar and salt and pepper. Cook gently for 2 minutes then add the spring onions and sesame oil. Tip into a warm serving dish and garnish with toasted sesame seeds.

OYSTERS

Kulhoe

Instead of the traditional lemon juice, try spooning a little of this Korean sauce over oysters before sucking them, with their juices, from their shells.

SERVES 4

12–24 oysters in the shell, opened

SAUCE

2 tbsp rice vinegar
1 tbsp *kochujang* (see below) or chilli bean paste
1cm/½in piece of fresh ginger, crushed and finely chopped
1½ tsp sugar
few drops of soy sauce to taste

❖ Mix together all the ingredients for the sauce, adjusting the levels of flavourings to taste. Pour into a small bowl. Cover and chill until ready to serve.

❖ Before serving, spoon the ready-made sauce over the oysters.

HOME-MADE RED PEPPER PASTE

Kochujang

Kochujang is an important seasoning and flavouring (see page 11). It used to be made at home, from home-fermented soya beans, but even in Korea it is often bought ready-made nowadays. In the West it can only be purchased from Korean shops but an approximation can be made at home quite easily using fairly readily available ingredients.

MAKES ABOUT 7 TBSP

4 tbsp brown or red miso
1½ tbsp paprika
1 tsp cayenne pepper
1 tbsp sugar

❖ Mix all the ingredients together in a small bowl. Keep in a screw-top jar in a cool, dark place, It will keep for up to six months in these conditions.

◀ *Oysters*

GRILLED SCALLOP KEBABS

Paejusanjok

Rice vinegar begins to "cook" the scallops in the same way that lime juice "cooks" fish when making Mexican *ceviche*, so the scallops need only brief cooking under the grill if they are not to become overcooked.

SERVES 2-4

12 large scallops
1 garlic clove, crushed and finely chopped
1 tbsp spring onion, green part, finely chopped
2 tbsp soy sauce
2 tsp rice vinegar
1 tbsp sesame oil
1cm/½in piece of fresh ginger, grated
2 tsp Crushed Toasted Sesame Seeds
(see page 22)
pinch of chilli powder

❖ Cut each scallop in half horizontally. Thread the scallops on to skewers and lay them in a shallow, non-metallic dish.

❖ Mix together the remaining ingredients and pour over the scallops. Turn the skewers over and leave for 15–30 minutes, turning occasionally.

❖ Pre-heat the grill.

❖ Lift the skewers from the marinade and cook under the grill for about 4 minutes, turning occasionally and brushing with the marinade.

STEAMED CRAB

Ke-tchim

The crab mixture can be steamed in a large crab shell. It is well worth using fresh crabmeat for better flavour and texture.

SERVES 6

50g/2oz beansprouts
40g/1 ½oz medium-firm bean curd
about 450g/1lb mixed white and brown crabmeat, finely chopped
1cm/½in piece of fresh ginger, grated
2 spring onions, very finely chopped
1 tsp sesame oil
salt and freshly ground black pepper
1 tbsp plain flour
1 egg, beaten
diagonally sliced white and green parts of spring onion for garnish

❖ Add the beansprouts to a saucepan of boiling water. Quickly return to the boil and boil for 1 minute. Tip into a colander and rinse under cold water. Drain well then squeeze out as much water as possible. Chop finely.

❖ Wrap the bean curd in a clean cloth and squeeze firmly to express surplus liquid. Finely crumble the bean curd. Mix the crabmeat, beansprouts, bean curd, ginger, spring onions, sesame oil and seasonings together. Divide between 6 individual heatproof dishes.

❖ Sift the flour over the tops of the dishes then brush with beaten egg. Put in a steaming basket. Cover the dishes with greaseproof paper and cover the steaming basket. Put the steaming basket over a saucepan of boiling water and steam the crab for about 10 minutes. Garnish with spring onions.

GRILLED FISH

Saengsongui

For this dish you can use red snapper, sea bass, pompano, grey mullet or trout. If preferred, fish steaks or cutlets can be used in place of a whole fish; there will be no need to slash these and they will only need to be cooked for 3–5 minutes a side, depending on thickness and type.

SERVES 2-4

675g/1 ½lb whole fish, scaled and cleaned
1 ½ tbsp rice vinegar
2 tbsp sesame oil
3 tbsp soy sauce
2 garlic cloves, crushed and finely chopped
2.5cm/1in piece of fresh ginger, grated
1 spring onion, white and green part finely sliced
1 ½ tbsp Crushed Toasted Sesame Seeds (see page 22)
2 tsp Korean chilli powder, or cayenne pepper mixed with paprika
2 tsp sugar
freshly ground black pepper

❖ With the point of a sharp knife cut four deep diagonal slashes on each side of the fish.

❖ Mix together the remaining ingredients and rub one third into the fish, taking care to work it deep into the slashes.

❖ Pre-heat the grill. Grill the fish about 15cm/6in away from the heat for 6–7 minutes a side, basting occasionally with another third of the sauce.

❖ Transfer the fish to a warm serving plate and pour over the remaining sauce.

FRIED FISH STRIPS

Saengsonjon

These are cut into strips similar to French *goujons*, but they are lighter to eat as they are coated in just egg and flour rather than batter, and shallow- rather than deep-fried.

SERVES 3-4

550g 1¼lb white fish fillets such as cod or plaice
1 plump garlic clove, halved lengthways
seasoned plain flour for coating
1–2 eggs, beaten
oil for frying
Seasoned Dipping Sauce (see page 75) to serve

❖ Rub the fish with the cut side of the garlic halves, then thinly slice the fish diagonally.

❖ Coat the fish in seasoned flour, then dip in beaten egg and allow excess egg to drain off.

❖ Heat a shallow layer of oil in a frying-pan, add the fish strips, in batches if necessary so they are not crowded, and fry for about 5 minutes, depending on thickness. Transfer to paper towels to drain then serve hot with Seasoned Dipping Sauce.

SEASONED DIPPING SAUCE

Yangyumjang

This version of *chojang* has the most complex flavours.

MAKES 7 TBSP

4 tbsp soy sauce
2 tsp sesame oil
1 tbsp rice vinegar
about 1/4–1/2 fresh red or green chilli
2 tsp toasted sesame seeds
pinch of sugar
1/2–1 small garlic clove, finely chopped

❖ Combine the soy sauce, sesame oil and rice vinegar in a small bowl. Deseed the chilli and chop finely. Add to the bowl with remaining ingredients and mix well.

KOREAN FISH STEW

Maeuctana

Like other great fish stew-soups of the world, such as *bouillabaisse*, this is made with a mixture of fish and shellfish that happen to be available.

SERVES 4

4 dried Chinese black mushrooms, soaked in 150ml/5fl oz hot water for 30 minutes
1.2 litres/2pt Korean Chicken Stock (see page 16)
675–800g/1 1/2–1 3/4lb whole fish, cut into large chunks or filleted and cut into 5cm/2in pieces
about 1 tbsp *kochujang* (see page 69) or chilli bean paste
2 tsp sesame oil
salt and freshly ground black pepper
4 spring onions, finely chopped
1 red pepper, chopped
12 fresh clams, cleaned
115g/4oz young fresh spinach leaves
diagonally sliced spring onion leaves and sesame oil to garnish

❖ Drain the mushrooms, reserving the liquid. Cut away and discard the mushroom stalks and slice the caps. Strain the reserved liquid into a saucepan. Add the fish pieces and the stock. Bring to the boil, skim off any scum, then simmer for 30 minutes. Strain the stock and return it to the saucepan. Add *kochujang* to taste. Lightly season the fish and sprinkle with the sesame oil. Leave for 30 minutes.

❖ Add the spring onions and red pepper to the stock. Bring to the boil and add the clams. Cook for about 2 minutes then add all the fish and spinach. Bring just to a simmer then cook gently for about 3 minutes, until the fish is opaque; discard any clams that remain closed. Garnish and serve.

PRAWNS IN JACKETS

Saeutigim

When raw, tiger prawns are dark greyish-brown with darker rings but the shells turn rosy pink and the flesh pale pinkish white when cooked. They are quite expensive but they are large and meaty – they can range from 7.5cm/3in up to enormous specimens of 30cm/10in – so three tiger prawns of about 7.5–10cm/3–4in are enough for one portion.

SERVES 4

75g/3oz plain flour
2 tsp black sesame seeds
salt and freshly ground black pepper
1 egg, beaten
1–2 tsp sesame oil
12 raw tiger prawns in their shells, about 7.5cm/3in long
vegetable oil for deep-frying
Vinegar Dipping Sauce (see page 32) to serve

❖ Stir together the flour, sesame seeds and seasoning. Stir in the egg and sesame oil, then add enough water (about 115ml/4fl oz) to make a light coating batter. Set aside.

❖ Remove the heads and fine legs from the prawns, leaving the tails intact. With a fine knife-point, slit along the back of each prawn and remove the dark thread.

❖ Half fill a deep-fat fryer with vegetable oil and heat to 180°C/350°F.

❖ Stir the batter, then dip the prawns into it. Allow excess batter to drain off the prawns, then deep-fry in batches for about 3–4 minutes until crisp and brown. Transfer to paper towels to drain. Keep warm while frying the remaining prawns. Serve hot with Vinegar Dipping Sauce.

now becoming more popular.

Chicken has for a long time been a mainstay of the Korean diet and there are many ways of cooking it.

QUICK BEEF

Pangjagui

The original concept of this recipe is that it is prepared and cooked quickly for people who are waiting to eat, but the beef can be marinated in a cool place with the remaining ingredients for 1–3 hours to give it extra flavour.

SERVES 2

225g/8oz rump steak
2 garlic cloves, crushed and finely chopped
2 spring onions, finely chopped
2 tbsp sesame oil
1 tbsp beef stock
salt and freshly ground black pepper

❖ Pre-heat the grill. Cut the beef across the grain into slices about 1cm/½in thick. Score the slices on both sides. Put into a bowl.

❖ Mix the remaining ingredients together, pour over the beef, stir to coat in the marinade then grill for 5–7 minutes, turning half-way through, until cooked to your liking.

PIQUANT LIVER

Kangui

This Korean treatment of liver makes it succulent, moist and tasty.

SERVES 2-4

225g/8oz lambs' liver, thinly sliced then cut into 4 x 2.5cm/1½ x 1in pieces
2 tbsp soy sauce
1 garlic clove, cut into fine slivers
1 tbsp sesame seeds
1 tsp sesame oil
about 1 tbsp sugar
freshly ground black pepper
1 large onion
1 spring onion, sliced and 25g/1oz mange tout for garnish

❖ Put the liver into a saucepan with the soy sauce, garlic, sesame seeds, sesame oil, sugar to taste and plenty of black pepper.

❖ Cut the onion into quarters then slice each quarter crossways into four slices. Add to the pan and cook over a medium heat, gently stirring occasionally, for 5 minutes.

❖ Add 150ml/5fl oz water to the pan and simmer very gently for about 5–8 minutes until the liver is tender.

❖ Garnish with spring onion and mange tout.

◀ *Piquant Liver*

BEEF AND VEGETABLE HOTPOT

Chongol

Chongol is a communal one-pot meal, every person dipping into the pot to select their chosen morsels. Any number of a wide variety of ingredients can be added, according to what is available, or to suit the occasion. Traditionally it is prepared over a burner at the table.

SERVES 4-6

- **550g/1¼lb sirloin or fillet of beef, partly frozen**
- **725ml/1¼pt brown veal or chicken stock**
- **6 celery stalks, cut into 5cm/2in pieces**
- **2 young carrots, finely sliced diagonally**
- **8 chestnut mushrooms**
- **8 spring onions, cut diagonally into 5cm/2in pieces**
- **6 Chinese leaves, cut into 5cm/2in pieces**
- **1½ cakes of bean curd, cut into 2.5cm/1in cubes**

MARINADE

- **2 teaspoons sesame seeds**
- **40g/1½oz sugar**
- **1 fresh red chilli, seeded and finely chopped**
- **6 tablespoons soy sauce**
- **1 plump garlic clove, finely crushed**

❖ For the marinade, heat a dry heavy-based saucepan, add the sesame seeds and toast until pale brown. Remove and crush finely. Mix with the remaining marinade ingredients.

❖ Slice the beef and cut into 2.5 x 5cm/1 x 2in strips. Put into a bowl, pour over the marinade and stir to coat. Leave for 1 hour.

❖ Heat a dry heavy-based pan. Remove the beef from the marinade and add to the pan. Cook briefly and quickly to sear the meat. Remove. Add the stock and any remaining marinade to the pan and bring to the boil. If using a fondue pot, boil the stock in a saucepan then pour into the fondue pot.

❖ Add the celery and carrots to the pot, boil for 5 minutes, then add the mushrooms, spring onions, Chinese leaves, bean curd and beef. Simmer together for 2–3 minutes then lower the heat so the stock gently simmers while the chongol is eaten.

BRAISED BEEF WITH CARROTS AND ONIONS

Kalbitchim I

The beef is marinated, then cooked slowly for a long time so that it can easily be removed from the bone with chopsticks.

SERVES 4

1.5kg/3lb beef short ribs
1½ tbsp vegetable oil
2 carrots, cut into chunks
1 onion, cut into chunks
sesame seeds, coriander and pine nuts for garnish

MARINADE

2 tbsp sesame oil
6 tbsp soy sauce
4 spring onions, white and green parts thinly sliced
4 tbsp rice wine or dry sherry
2 tbsp Crushed Toasted Sesame Seeds **(see page 22)**
2.5cm/1in piece of fresh ginger, finely chopped
3 garlic cloves, crushed and finely chopped
freshly ground black pepper

❖ Separate the beef into individual ribs and cut each one into 5cm/2in lengths. Make four deep slashes in a lattice pattern on the meaty sides of each piece of rib, going right through to the bone. Put into a bowl. Add the marinade ingredients, stir together well then cover and leave in a cool place for 4 hours, stirring the beef occasionally.

❖ Remove the beef from the marinade; reserve the marinade.

❖ Heat the vegetable oil in a heavy flameproof casserole and fry the beef for 5 minutes. Add the onion and carrot chunks and fry for a further 3 minutes. Pour in the reserved marinade and add enough water just to cover the beef and vegetables. Bring to the boil, cover and simmer gently for 1½–2 hours, turning the beef and vegetables occasionally, until the beef is very tender. Uncover the casserole about half to three-quarters of the way through the cooking so the sauce reduces.

❖ At the end of the cooking boil the sauce hard to reduce it to a thickish syrup, turning the ribs to make sure they are evenly coated. Skim any fat from the surface and serve garnished with pine nuts, sesame seeds and coriander.

BRAISED BEEF WITH WHITE RADISH

Kalbitchim 2

By the end of the cooking the pieces or rib and radish are coated in a thick, rich sauce.

SERVES 4

1.5kg/3lb beef short ribs
450g/1lb white radish, cut into 5cm/2in cubes
450ml/15fl oz water
8 dried Chinese black mushrooms
4–6 garlic cloves, crushed
5 tbsp soy sauce
1 tbsp sesame oil
2 tbsp Crushed Toasted Sesame Seeds (see page 22)
2 tbsp light brown sugar
freshly ground black pepper

❖ Separate the beef into individual ribs and cut each one into 5cm/2in lengths. Make four deep slashes in a lattice pattern on the meaty sides of each piece of rib, going right through to the bone. Add to a large saucepan of boiling water. Bring the water to the boil again, boil for 1 minute then drain the beef and rinse under running cold water.

❖ Put the beef and white radish in a large frying-pan, add the water and bring to the boil. Cover and simmer gently for 40 minutes.

❖ Meanwhile, soak the Chinese mushrooms in hot water for about 20 minutes. Lift the mushrooms from the water with a slotted spoon and cut off and discard any hard parts and the hard stems.

❖ Add the garlic, soy sauce, sesame oil, sesame seeds, sugar and plenty of pepper to the beef. Raise the heat and bring to the boil again. Lower the heat to moderately low and cook for 20 minutes with the lid slightly off.

❖ Turn the beef and radish in the sauce, add the mushrooms and continue to cook, partially covered, for a further 30 minutes, basting occasionally, or until the beef is tender.

❖ Remove the lid, raise the heat and cook until the sauce is reduced to a few spoonfuls.

STIR-FRIED BEEF WITH GARLIC AND CHILLIES

Soegogochubokkum

Garlic and chillies give the character to this simple, tasty stir-fry but the number of each can be adjusted according to personal taste.

SERVES 3-4

450g/1lb sirloin steak, cut into strips
2 tbsp soy sauce
1 spring onion, white and green part thinly sliced
1½ tsp sesame oil
2 tbsp rice wine or dry sherry
1½ tsp sugar
1½ tbsp vegetable oil
3 garlic cloves, cut into slivers
4 fresh red chillies, seeded and cut into strips
½ egg, beaten, fried and cut into strips (see below) for garnish
toasted sesame seeds for garnish

❖ Put the beef in a bowl, add the soy sauce, spring onion, sesame oil, rice wine or dry sherry and sugar. Stir, then cool for 1 hour.

❖ Heat the oil in a frying-pan. Add the garlic and chillies and stir-fry over a high heat until fragrant, about 1 minute. Remove with a slotted spoon and reserve.

❖ Lift the beef from the marinade, add to the pan and stir-fry for 2–3 minutes. Return the chillies and garlic to the pan, add the marinade and cook, stirring, over a moderate heat for about 2 minutes. Serve garnished with egg strips and toasted sesame seeds.

FRIED EGG STRIP GARNISH

Chon

A common garnish for Korean savoury dishes. Lightly beaten eggs are fried one at a time to keep the mixture thin. Sometimes, the eggs are separated and the yolks and whites cooked separately.

SERVES 1

1 egg, lightly beaten
vegetable oil for frying

❖ Heat a very thin film of vegetable oil in a large frying-pan, preferably non-stick. Pour in the egg and tilt and swirl the pan to spread the egg out in a thin even layer. Fry for 1–2 minutes until set underneath, then turn the "omelette" over and fry until set. Transfer the "omelette" to a wooden board, or a work surface and roll it up. Cut into 5mm/¼in strips.

QUICK-COOK BEEF, BEAN CURD AND VEGETABLE "STEW"

Twoenjangchigae

Richness and depth is given to the flavour of this "stew" by making the stock with *twoenjang*, Korean fermented bean curd. The beef is then cooked for just 2 minutes.

SERVES 3-4

225g/8oz sirloin or rump steak, cut into 2.5 x 5cm/ 1 x 2in slices
2 tsp sesame oil
1½ tsp sugar
freshly ground black pepper
8 dried Chinese black mushrooms, soaked in hot water for 30 minutes drained, and stalks removed
1 onion, thinly sliced into rings
1 courgette, sliced
2 spring onions, white and green parts sliced
1–2 fresh red chillies, seeded and thickly sliced
2 x 115g/4oz cakes of medium-firm bean curd, cut into 4cm/1½in chunks

STOCK

8 tbsp *twoenjang* (fermented bean curd) or miso
2 garlic cloves, lightly crushed
1 onion, cut into chunks
1 carrot, cut into chunks
3 spring onions, white and green parts cut into 7.5cm/ 3in lengths

❖ Put the *twoenjang* or miso in a sieve placed over a saucepan. Slowly pour through 950ml/32fl oz of water, pushing the *twoenjang* or miso with the back of a wooden spoon so it is all pushed through. Add the remaining stock ingredients and bring to the boil. Cover and simmer gently for 30 minutes.

❖ Meanwhile, mix the beef with the sesame oil, sugar and plenty of black pepper. Leave for 30 minutes.

❖ Strain the stock, squeezing out as much liquid as possible. Pour the stock back into the pan and add the mushroom caps, onion, courgette, spring onions and chillies. Bring to the boil then simmer for 2 minutes. Add the beef slices to the stock with the bean curd. Return to the boil, then simmer for 2 minutes.

BEEF AND BEAN CURD PATTIES

Gogijon

These light patties are served as simple everyday fare in most Korean homes. The patties are usually small so that they can be lifted with the slim Korean chopsticks.

SERVES 4-6

225g/8oz medium-firm bean curd
350g/12oz lean beef, freshly minced
2 garlic cloves, crushed and finely chopped
2 spring onions, white and green parts very finely chopped
1 tbsp sesame oil
2 tsp soy sauce
4 tsp Crushed Toasted Sesame Seeds (see page 22)
plain flour for coating
2 eggs, beaten
vegetable oil for frying

❖ Put the bean curd in a piece of muslin or fine cloth and squeeze out as much water as possible. Press the bean curd through a sieve then mix with the beef, garlic, spring onions, sesame oil, soy sauce and sesame seeds. Form into patties about 4cm/$1\frac{1}{2}$in in diameter and just under 1cm/$\frac{1}{2}$in thick.

❖ Toss the patties in plain flour to coat evenly then dip in beaten egg.

❖ Heat a thin layer of vegetable oil in a large frying-pan. Add some of the patties to make a single layer and fry slowly for $2\frac{1}{2}$–3 minutes a side or until golden. Using a slotted spoon transfer the patties to paper towels to drain while frying the remaining patties.

KOREAN MEATBALLS

Sogoki-chun

These flavourful meatballs are served as one of the side dishes in a Korean meal. They are also good cold so a useful item for a picnic.

SERVES 2-3

225g/8oz lean minced beef
3 tbsp soy sauce
2 spring onions, finely chopped
2 garlic cloves, finely chopped
1 tbsp Crushed Toasted Sesame Seeds (see page 22)
1½ tsp sesame oil
freshly ground black pepper
seasoned plain flour for coating
2 eggs, lightly beaten
vegetable oil for frying
Vinegar Dipping Sauce (see page 32) to serve

❖ Mix together the beef, soy sauce, spring onions, garlic, sesame seeds, sesame oil and plenty of pepper. Leave for 30 minutes.

❖ Form the meat mixture into flattened circles about 4cm/1½in in diameter. Toss in seasoned flour to coat evenly then dip in beaten egg, allowing excess egg to drain off.

❖ Heat a little oil in a frying-pan, preferably non-stick, and fry the meatballs until brown and crisp on both sides and cooked through.

❖ Serve with Vinegar Dipping Sauce.

GRILLED STEAK WITH SESAME

Tungshimgui

This is a very quick, simple treatment for well-flavoured sirloin steak. Use good quality meat and preferably meat that has not been frozen.

SERVES 3-4

1 or 2 pieces of sirloin steak, total weight about 675g/1½lb, well chilled
1 garlic clove, crushed
2 tbsp sesame oil
1 tbsp toasted sesame seeds
salt

❖ Using a large, sharp knife, thinly slice the sirloin diagonally across the grain. Rub each slice with garlic and brush with sesame oil.

❖ Pre-heat the grill or barbecue. Grill or barbecue the beef for 1–2 minutes a side. Sprinkle with sesame seeds and salt and serve.

KOREAN "HOT MEAT"

Changjorim

The beef is served cold with its own spicy jelly as a side dish, and is eaten in small amounts. Because the jelly is an integral part of the dish it is important to use a gelatinous cut of beef, such as shin. Adjust the number of chillies to suit your taste for "hot" foods.

SERVES 4-6

900g/2lb shin of beef
3 tbsp sesame oil
6 tbsp Japanese soy sauce
about 8 fresh red or green chillies, halved and seeded
1 red pepper, seeded and quite thinly sliced

❖ Put the meat into a saucepan, add enough water just to cover it and bring to the boil. Skim the scum from the surface then add the remaining ingredients. Cover the pan and simmer very gently for 2–3 hours until the meat is so tender it is beginning to fall apart. Keep an eye on the water level to make sure the pan does not become dry but do not drown the meat. At the end of the cooking it should be surrounded by a thick sauce.

❖ Remove from the heat and leave the meat to cool in the liquid. Break the meat apart with a fork and serve with the jelly, chillies and sliced red pepper.

GRILLED BEEF

Pulgogi

Pulgogi is one of the most popular Korean dishes. Pulgogi is also the name of the domed-shape metal hotplate that is put on a table-top burner for cooking the beef. A grill and grill rack or a barbecue can be used instead.

SERVES 4

4 spring onions, coarsely chopped
3 garlic cloves, crushed and finely chopped
1 tbsp Crushed Toasted Sesame Seeds (see page 22)
3 tbsp soy sauce
2 tsp rice wine or dry sherry
1 tbsp sesame oil
2 tbsp sugar
freshly ground black pepper
550g/1 ¼lb fillet, sirloin or rump of beef, frozen for 1 hour
vegetable oil for brushing

❖ Mix together the spring onions, garlic, sesame seeds, soy sauce, rice wine or sherry, sesame oil, sugar, 2 tablespoons water and plenty of black pepper.

❖ Cut the beef crossways into 5mm/¼in thick slices. Lay in a shallow dish. Pour over the spring onion mixture, cover and leave to marinate for 1 hour.

❖ Pre-heat the grill or barbecue (depending on what you are using). Lightly oil a grill rack or table-top grill plate. Cook the beef in batches in a single layer for about 1 minute a side until browned on the outside but still pink inside.

ABOVE *Lush, green countryside is often the result of long, hot summers and plenty of rain.*

SPICED BARBECUED BEEF RIBS

Kalbigui

Beef, or pork, spare ribs can be used instead of beef short ribs. The traditional accompaniments are rice, a *kimchi* (see pages 40–64) and a selection of salads.

SERVES 4

900g/2lb beef short ribs, cut into 7.5cm/3in lengths
1 tbsp Crushed Toasted Sesame Seeds (see page 22)
4 tbsp Japanese soy sauce
4 spring onions, white parts only, sliced and crushed
3 garlic cloves, crushed and finely chopped
1½ tbsp sesame oil
2.5cm/1in piece of fresh ginger, grated
2 tsp sugar
freshly ground black pepper
toasted sesame seeds for garnish

❖ Using a sharp knife, cut the meaty sides of the ribs through to the bone in a lattice pattern. This allows the marinade to penetrate, tenderizes the meat and hastens the cooking. Put the ribs into a dish.

❖ Mix together the remaining ingredients, except the garnish, and pour over the meat. Stir to mix, then cover and leave for at least 3–4 hours, preferably overnight.

❖ Pre-heat the grill or barbecue.

❖ Lift the beef from the marinade. Grill or barbecue the beef, brushing occasionally with the marinade, until it's a rich golden brown, 12–15 minutes each side. Serve hot sprinkled with sesame seeds.

ABOVE *Ceremony plays a large part in Korean life; respect for elders, religious events, and here, tea drinking.*

叉燒飽
宮保蝦仁
揚州炒飯

KOREAN BRAISED CHICKEN THIGHS

Takpokkum

Chicken thighs become richly flavoured and very tender and succulent when steeped in a tasty marinade, then fried and braised in it.

SERVES 4

8 chicken thighs
4 spring onions, white parts only, very finely chopped
2.5cm/1in piece of fresh ginger, grated
2 garlic cloves, crushed and chopped
4 tbsp soy sauce
1 tbsp sesame oil
1½ tbsp Crushed Toasted Sesame Seeds **(see page 22)**
2 tsp sugar
vegetable oil for frying
1 red pepper, seeded and diced
2 spring onions, white and pale green parts sliced diagonally

❖ Slash each chicken thigh three times and place in a shallow dish.

❖ Mix together the finely chopped spring onions, ginger, garlic, soy sauce, sesame oil, sesame seeds and sugar. Pour over the chicken, turn to coat with the sauce and leave in a cool place for about 4 hours, turning occasionally.

❖ Heat a little vegetable oil in a heavy flameproof casserole. Lift the chicken thighs from the marinade, add to the casserole and brown evenly. Pour in the marinade and enough water just to cover the chicken. Bring barely to simmering point, cover the casserole and leave to cook gently for about 30–35 minutes, turning the chicken occasionally, until very tender.

❖ Add the red pepper and sliced spring onions about 5 minutes before the end of cooking. If necessary, uncover the casserole towards the end of cooking to allow the sauce to reduce.

MARINATED THINLY SLICED CHICKEN BREAST

Takkooe

Traditionally, vegetables, rice and pickles are served with the chicken but I also like to eat it with a crisp salad, or on firm white, crusty bread.

SERVES 3-4

- **3 tbsp Japanese dark soy sauce**
- **2 tbsp sesame oil**
- **1 tbsp Crushed Toasted Sesame Seeds (see page 22)**
- **2.5cm/1in piece fresh ginger, grated**
- **2 garlic cloves, crushed**
- **2 spring onions, white and green parts thinly sliced into rings**
- **2 tbsp rice wine or dry sherry**
- **salt and freshly ground black pepper**
- **350g/12oz skinned and boned chicken breast, chilled**
- **2 tbsp vegetable oil**
- **2 fresh hot red chillies, thickly sliced crossways**
- **4 large brown mushrooms, oyster or shiitake, each cut into 4 slices**

❖ Mix together the soy sauce, sesame oil and seeds, ginger, garlic, spring onions, rice wine or sherry, salt and plenty of black pepper to taste.

❖ Holding the knife at a slight angle, cut across the chicken breasts to make 3mm/⅛in wide slices. Using a meat mallet or the flat side of a cleaver, pound each slice, at the same time dragging the mallet or cleaver across the slice. Lay the slices in a large, shallow dish, pouring some of the soy/sesame sauce over each layer. Cover and leave for 1 hour.

❖ Heat the vegetable oil in a large, preferably non-stick, frying-pan. Lift some of the chicken slices from the marinade and add to the pan so they lie flat in a single layer. Cook for 1 minute on each side until lightly browned and cooked through. Transfer to a warm plate and keep warm while frying the remaining chicken.

❖ When all the chicken has been cooked, add the chillies, mushrooms and remaining marinade to the pan. Stir and cook for 1 minute. Pour over the chicken and serve immediately.

STIR-FRIED CHICKEN

Tak

Prepare the vegetables while the chicken is marinating then, once you start cooking, the recipe is soon ready to serve.

SERVES 4

450g/1lb skinned and boned chicken breasts, cut into strips
2 tbsp soy sauce
1 tbsp sugar
2 spring onions, white and some green parts finely chopped
2.5cm/1in piece of fresh ginger, finely chopped
1½ tsp Crushed Toasted Sesame Seeds (see page 22)
freshly ground black pepper
1 small carrot, thinly sliced diagonally
3 dried Chinese black mushrooms, soaked for 30 minutes in hot water
1½ tbsp sesame oil
1 red pepper, seeded and cut into thin strips
Fried Egg Strip Garnish (see page 85)

❖ Put the chicken into a bowl.

❖ Mix together the soy sauce, sugar, spring onions, ginger, sesame seeds and plenty of pepper. Pour over the chicken, turn the chicken over and leave for 30 minutes. Remove from the marinade; reserve the marinade.

❖ Meanwhile, blanch the carrot in boiling water for 5 minutes. Drain and set aside.

❖ Drain the mushrooms, cut out and discard any hard patches and the stalks. Slice the mushroom caps.

❖ Heat the sesame oil in a frying-pan, add the chicken and stir-fry for 2–3 minutes, remove from pan and set aside. Add the mushrooms and carrots, stir-fry for 2 minutes then add the pepper and stir-fry for another minute.

❖ Return the chicken to the pan, add the reserved marinade and bring to the boil. Stir and cook for 1 minute then serve garnished with egg strips.

CHICKEN AND SPRING ONION KEBABS

Taksanjok

As good as these kebabs are when grilled they are even better when cooked on a barbecue.

SERVES 4

about 675g/1½lb skinned and boned chicken thighs
1–2 bunches plump spring onions, white parts only
4 tbsp soy sauce
1 tbsp sesame oil
2 tsp sugar
2 garlic cloves, crushed and finely chopped
2cm/¾in piece of fresh ginger, grated
1 tbsp Crushed Toasted Sesame Seeds (see page 22)
diagonally sliced pale green parts of spring onion for garnish
toasted sesame seeds for garnish

❖ Cut each chicken thigh into three lengths. Thread pieces of chicken and spring onions alternately on to short skewers. Lay the skewers in a large, shallow dish.

❖ Mix together the remaining ingredients, except the garnishes, and pour over the skewers. Turn to coat with the sauce then leave for 3–4 hours, turning occasionally.

❖ Pre-heat the grill or barbecue.

❖ Lift the skewers from the marinade and grill or barbecue for about 10–15 minutes, turning occasionally and brushing with the remaining marinade. Serve garnished with spring onions and toasted sesame seeds.

The traditional rhythm of the Korean year revolves around the ritual planting and harvesting of rice. Rice is the basic foodstuff of Koreans, and in per capita terms, their annual rice consumption is among the world's highest.

Rice is served, in small metal bowls, as the essential accompaniment to every meal; in hard times it is especially valuable for adding bulk to otherwise meagre meals.

Noodles, which are regarded as a symbol of longevity, are also popular; noodle stalls are found on many town street corners. As well as noodles made from wheat flour, there are noodles made from buckwheat and mung bean flour.

Bean curd is an important food in the Korean diet. It is bought fresh every day from door-to-door salesmen, or made at home.

BOILED RICE

Ssalbap

Boiled rice not only provides a foundation for other dishes but is enjoyed on its own. For authentic results it is important to use the correct fat, short-grained variety – "Kokuho Rose" is a good brand to search for in ethnic shops. If you want to cook a different quantity of rice simply follow the volume formula of rice to water – 1:1¼. Korean rice is never salted as the foods with which it is eaten are already sufficiently salty.

SERVES 4-6

short-grained rice measured to the 450ml/15fl oz mark in a measuring jug

❖ Put the rice in a large bowl and add water to cover it generously. Swish the rice around with your hand, at the same time rubbing the grains. When the water has become milky white, pour it away. Repeat the washing several times until the water is virtually clear. Leave the rice to soak for 2–3 hours. Tip the rice into a sieve and leave to drain and dry for 1 hour.

❖ Put the rice into a heavy-based saucepan, add 575ml/1pt water and bring to the boil. Stir once, cover, turn the heat right down and cook the rice for 20 minutes, without removing the lid even once. Turn the heat up as high as it will go for 30 seconds then turn it off, or remove the pan from the heat. Leave, without removing the lid at all, for 10–15 minutes before serving.

RICE WITH MILLET

Kijangbap

Traditionally, Kijangbap was prepared for the same reasons as Poribap (see page 103). A nuttier flavour can be obtained by toasting the millet, prior to boiling, in a dry saucepan over a moderate heat for 3 minutes.

SERVES 2-4

short-grained rice measured to the 350ml/12fl oz mark in a measuring jug, washed and soaked (see above)
115g/4oz millet

❖ Put the rice and millet into a saucepan. Add 720ml/1¼pt water and bring to the boil. Stir once, cover, turn the heat right down and cook the rice for 20 minutes, without removing the lid even once. Turn the heat up as high as it will go for 30 seconds then turn it off, or remove the pan from the heat. Leave, without removing the lid at all, for 10–15 minutes before serving.

RICE AND MUSHROOMS

Posotbap

Using mushrooms (of which Koreans are very fond) with a small amount of beef to flavour rice is a good way of boosting the meaty flavour and giving the illusion that there is more meat than there actually is.

SERVES 3-4

150g/5oz lean minced beef
225g/8oz open-cap mushrooms, preferably brown cap, chopped
2 garlic cloves, crushed and finely chopped
2 spring onions, white and some green parts, chopped
2 tbsp soy sauce
1 ½ tsp sesame oil
1 tbsp Crushed Toasted Sesame Seeds (see page 22)
freshly ground black pepper
2 tsp vegetable oil
short-grain white rice measured to the 225ml/8fl oz mark on a measuring jug, washed and soaked (see page 102)
very fine slices of red chilli for garnish

❖ Mix together the beef, mushrooms, garlic, spring onions, soy sauce, sesame oil, sesame seeds and plenty of pepper. Leave for at least 30 minutes.

❖ Heat the vegetable oil in a saucepan, add the mushroom and beef mixture and stir until the beef just changes colour. Stir in the rice and 300ml/10fl oz water. Cover and bring to the boil. Stir once and cover again. Turn the heat to very low and cook for 20–30 minutes, without removing the lid even once. Turn the heat up as high as it will go for 30 seconds then turn it off, or remove the pan from the heat. Leave, without removing the lid at all, for 10–15 minutes. Stir before serving garnished with very fine slices of red chilli.

RICE WITH BARLEY

Poribap

Barley used to be added to rice towards the end of summer when rice stocks were getting low, to eke it out until the next crop was harvested.

SERVES 4

short-grained rice measured to the 350ml/12fl oz mark in a measuring jug, washed and soaked (see page 102)
115g/4oz pearl barley

❖ Put the rice and pearl barley into a saucepan. Add 720ml/1 ¼pt water and bring to the boil. Stir once, cover, turn the heat right down and cook the rice for about 20 minutes, without removing the lid even once. Continue as in recipe for Rice with Millet (see page 102).

RICE WITH SPINACH, BEANSPROUTS AND LAVER

Pibimbap

This dish is generally eaten with a dipping sauce.

SERVES 4-6

225g/8oz young fresh spinach, cut across into 2cm/¾in strips
225g/8oz mung beansprouts
1 garlic clove, chopped
1 carrot, cut into fine strips
2 spring onions, white and green parts sliced diagonally
1½ sheets *kim* (*nori* or laver), cut into thin strips
2 tsp sesame oil
3 tbsp soy sauce
2 tsp Crushed Toasted Sesame Seeds (see page 22)
½ tsp sugar
freshly ground black pepper
short-grain rice measured to 450ml/15fl oz level in a measuring jug, washed and soaked (see page 102)

❖ Add the spinach and beansprouts to a large saucepan of water. Cover and quickly return to the boil. Boil for 1 minute then tip into a colander. Drain well then squeeze out as much water as possible. Mix with the remaining ingredients except the rice and leave for 30 minutes.

❖ Drain the rice and put into a saucepan with the vegetable mixture and 575ml/1pt water. Stir, then cover and bring to the boil. Stir once, cover again, and turn the heat to very low and cook for 20–30 minutes, without removing the lid even once. Turn the heat up as high as it will go for 30 seconds then turn it off, or remove the pan from the heat. Leave, without removing the lid at all, for 10–15 minutes before serving.

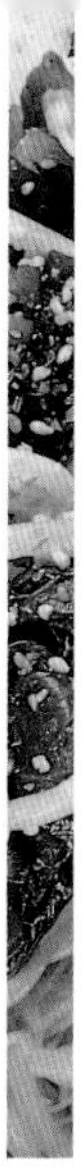

COLD NOODLES WITH VEGETABLES

Kuksu

This is a vegetarian version of Kuksu, a popular noodle dish which is served surrounded by small bowls of condiments, relishes and side dishes, the most important of which are soy sauce, Korean chilli powder, and *kimchis* (see pages 40–64). If you are unable to buy *son myon* noodles which are available from Korean food shops, use vermicelli and cook according to the directions on the packet.

SERVES 4

3 tbsp soy sauce
1 tbsp sugar
1 tbsp sesame oil
5 dried Chinese black mushrooms, soaked for 30 minutes in hot water
115g/4oz beansprouts
450g/1lb young fresh spinach leaves, stalks removed
450ml/15fl oz vegetable stock
225g/8oz *son myon* noodles or vermicelli
green part of 1 spring onion, diagonally sliced
1 tbsp Crushed Toasted Sesame Seeds (see page 22)
very small pinch of Korean chilli powder, or cayenne pepper mixed with paprika

❖ Mix together 2 tablespoons of the soy sauce, 2 teaspoons of the sugar and the sesame oil.

❖ Drain the mushrooms and cut out and discard the stalks and any woody parts. Thinly slice the caps.

❖ Bring 750ml/1¼pt water to the boil in a saucepan and add the remaining sugar. Put the beansprouts into a sieve and lower the sieve into the water. Return the water to the boil and cook the beansprouts for 20 seconds. Remove the sieve of beansprouts from the water and rinse them under running cold water. Leave to drain completely.

❖ Add the spinach to the saucepan and boil for 2 minutes or until wilted. Drain, rinse under running cold water and drain again.

❖ Pour the stock into a saucepan, add the remaining soy sauce and bring to the boil. Add the noodles and boil for about 3 minutes until just tender. Quickly remove the noodles from the water using a slotted spoon and put into a warm serving dish. Add the spinach and mushrooms to the liquid, heat through then quickly remove, season with the soy sauce mixture and pile on to the noodles. Keep warm.

❖ Heat the beansprouts in the stock then remove and quickly season with the remaining soy sauce mixture. Place on top of the spinach and mushrooms. Pour the remaining stock around the noodles and sprinkle with the spring onion, sesame seeds and a little chilli powder or cayenne mixed with paprika.

CELLOPHANE NOODLES WITH VEGETABLES

Chapchae

Chapchae is a colourful vegetable-packed noodle dish with a multitude of different textures. Once the vegetables have been prepared it is very quick to assemble and cook.

SERVES 4

6 dried Chinese black mushrooms, soaked in hot water for 30 minutes
150g/5oz young fresh spinach leaves
2 Chinese cabbage leaves
3 shiitake or oyster mushrooms, thinly sliced
4 spring onions, white and green parts thickly sliced diagonally
1 small courgette, cut into fine strips
1 carrot, cut into fine strips
4 tbsp vegetable oil
1 tbsp sesame oil
3 garlic cloves, crushed and finely chopped
2 small fresh red chillies, seeded and cut into fine strips
50g/2oz cellophane noodles, soaked for 30 minutes and drained
1 tbsp soy sauce
1 tsp sugar
salt

❖ Drain the dried mushrooms and cut away and discard the stems and any hard parts. Thinly slice the mushroom caps.

❖ Add the spinach to a large saucepan of boiling water. Cover and quickly return to the boil. Boil for 2 minutes then drain and rinse under running cold water. Drain well and squeeze out as much water as possible. Separate the leaves.

❖ Cut away and discard the curly outer part of the Chinese cabbage leaves, saving only the "V" shaped core of the leaves. Cut this into fine strips then mix with the spinach, dried and fresh mushrooms, spring onions, courgette and carrot until well mixed.

❖ Heat the vegetable oil and sesame oil in a deep frying-pan, add the garlic and chilli and stir-fry for 10 seconds. Add the mixed vegetables and stir-fry for 3–4 minutes until the vegetables are tender but still crisp. Turn the heat to low and stir in the noodles, soy sauce, sugar and salt. Cook for 2 minutes then serve.

RICE WITH BEEF AND BEANSPROUTS

Kongamulbap

This is a dish eaten by poorer people as adding beef and beansprouts to plain rice makes the meat go further.

SERVES 3-4

2 tbsp soy sauce
2 garlic cloves, crushed and chopped
2 spring onions, white and a little green part finely chopped
1½ tbsp Crushed Toasted Sesame Seeds (see page 22)
1 tbsp sesame oil
freshly ground black pepper
150g/5oz lean beef, chilled
1 tbsp vegetable oil
short-grained rice measured to the 225ml/8fl oz mark in a measuring jug, washed, soaked and drained (see page 102)
225g/8oz beansprouts
very thin strips of red chilli for garnish

❖ Mix the soy sauce, garlic, spring onions, sesame seeds, sesame oil and pepper in a bowl.

❖ Slice the beef very thinly, stack the slices and cut into strips. Stir into the bowl with the soy mixture to coat evenly and leave for 1 hour, stirring two or three times.

❖ Heat the vegetable oil in a large saucepan, add the beef and stir-fry for 2–3 minutes until darker brown. Stir in the rice and beansprouts then add 350ml/12fl oz water. Bring to the boil. Stir once, cover, turn the heat to very low and cook the rice for 20 minutes, without removing the lid even once. Turn the heat up as high as it will go for 30 seconds then turn it off, or remove the pan from the heat. Leave, without removing the lid at all, for 10–15 minutes. Serve garnished with very thin strips of red chilli.

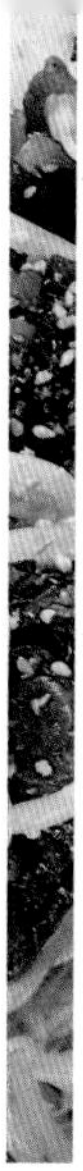

RICE WITH SOYA BEANSPROUTS

Kongnamulbab

The beansprouts provide a crisp contrast to the softness of the rice.

SERVES 4-6

225g/8oz soya beansprouts.
short-grain rice measured to the 450ml/15fl oz measure in a measuring jug, washed and soaked (see page 102)

❖ Add the beansprouts to a saucepan of boiling water, cover and quickly return to the boil. Boil for 2 minutes, then drain.

❖ Drain the rice and put it into a saucepan. Put the beansprouts on top and pour in 575ml/1pt water. Cover and bring to the boil. Stir once and cover again. Turn the heat to very low and cook for 20–30 minutes, without removing the lid. Turn the heat up high for 30 seconds then turn it off. Leave for 10–15 minutes before serving.

BEANS WITH MIXED GRAINS

Ogokbap

The combination of red and black beans and three different grains make this a colourful dish with many different tastes and textures.

SERVES 4

50g/2oz red kidney beans, soaked overnight
50g/2oz black kidney beans, soaked overnight
short-grained rice measured to the 225ml/8fl oz mark in a measuring jug, washed and soaked (see page 102)
25g/1oz millet
25g/1oz pearl barley

❖ Drain the beans, add to a saucepan of boiling water, cover and bring to the boil. Boil for 10 minutes, then simmer for 1–1½ hours until just tender; the time will depend on the beans. Drain them, reserving the water.

❖ Drain the rice. Put all the ingredients in a saucepan, add 400ml/14fl oz of the bean cooking water and bring to the boil. Stir once, then cover and turn the heat to very low. Cook for 20–30 minutes, without removing the lid even once. Turn the heat up as high as it will go for 30 seconds then turn it off, or remove the pan from the heat. Leave, without removing the lid at all, for 10–15 minutes before serving.

◀ *Beans with Mixed Grains*

FRESH BEAN CURD

Sundubu

Fresh bean curd, which is as white and soft as the white of poached eggs, is not difficult to make.

SERVES 4

350g/12oz yellow soya beans, soaked overnight
juice of 2 lemons

❖ Drain the beans and put half of them in a blender or food processor with 600ml/1pt warm water. Mix to a smooth purée. Pour the contents of the blender or food processor into a fine sieve lined with a large piece of muslin and placed over a large bowl.

❖ Repeat with the remaining beans and another 600ml/1pt warm water, adding the purée to the sieve. Fold the muslin over the pulp in the sieve and press firmly to extract as much liquid as possible.

❖ Return the residue in the sieve to the blender or food processor and add another 600ml/1pt warm water. Mix again for a couple of minutes then pour into the sieve to drain. Discard the residue in the sieve. The thickish white liquid is soya milk.

❖ Bring the soya milk to the boil in a large saucepan. As soon as it begins to rise in the pan, lower the heat and simmer the milk, uncovered, for 15–20 minutes, stirring occasionally.

❖ Remove from the heat and stir in the lemon juice, which should make the milk curdle. Pour the curds and liquid into a fine sieve lined with a large clean piece of muslin, and leave to strain.

❖ To make medium-firm bean curd, fold the muslin over the curds, cover the surface of the curd with a weight (a heavy saucepan will do) and leave to drain for 15 minutes. To make firm bean curd leave to drain for 2 hours. It will keep for up to two days, if covered with water and refrigerated.

ABOVE *The autumn harvest is a very important time of year, since winters tend to be long and often harsh.*

BRAISED BEAN CURD WITH PORK

Tubujorim I

This is another family way of braising bean curd.

SERVES 4

2 tbsp soy sauce
1 tsp sesame seeds
2 tbsp sugar
1 ½ tbsp *kochujang* (see page 69) or chilli bean paste
2 garlic cloves, crushed and finely chopped
2.5cm/1in piece of fresh ginger, grated
1 ½ tsp Crushed Toasted Sesame Seeds (see page 22)
350g/12oz lean pork loin, very thinly sliced on the diagonal
3 tbsp vegetable oil
2 x 115g/4oz cakes of medium-firm bean curd
spring onions, shredded diagonally for garnish

❖ Mix together the soy sauce, sesame seeds, sugar, *kochujang*, garlic and ginger.

❖ Lay the pork slices in a shallow dish and pour over the soy sauce mixture. Coat the pork with the mixture and leave for 30 minutes.

❖ Heat half the vegetable oil in a frying-pan, add the pork mixture and cook for 12–15 minutes, turning the pork half-way through, until cooked through. Add a little water, as necessary, to keep the mixture fairly liquid.

❖ Meanwhile, cut each bean curd cake horizontally in half then cut across each half into three pieces. Fry in the remaining oil in another frying-pan for about 3 minutes a side, until golden. Transfer to paper towels.

❖ Pour the oil from the second frying-pan then make a layer of bean curd in the pan. Cover with some of the pork mixture. Repeat, then cover and heat through gently for 5 minutes. Serve garnished with spring onions.

POACHED BEAN CURD

Tofu

This plainly cooked bean curd can be eaten as it comes, or served with a dipping sauce. The role of cooking liquid in the serving dish is to keep the bean curd hot; it is not drunk. If preferred, the bean curd can be served in individual dishes with seaweed and bonito flakes.

SERVES 4

12½g/½oz wakame
3 cakes of medium-firm bean curd, each about 115g/4oz
Vinegar Dipping Sauce (see page 32) to serve (optional)

❖ Bring 2.5 litres/4½pt water to the boil in a wide saucepan. Add the wakame and bean curd and simmer gently for 5 minutes.

❖ Using a slotted spoon, transfer the bean curd to a warm serving dish deep enough to allow the cakes to be almost covered by the cooking liquid. Pour in simmering cooking liquid to come three-quarters of the way up the sides of the bean curd cakes. Serve straightaway, accompanied by vinegar dipping sauce, if liked.

FRIED BEAN CURD

Tububuchim

A little sesame oil adds a subtle yet distinctive flavour that "lifts" simple fried bean curd.

SERVES 6

4 x 115g/4oz cakes of medium-firm bean curd
vegetable and sesame oil for frying
Vinegar Dipping Sauce (see page 32) to serve

❖ Cut the bean curd into rectangles approximately 4 x 2 x 2cm/1½ x ¾ x ¾in. Dry on paper towels.

❖ Heat a thin film of vegetable oil mixed with a little sesame oil in a non-stick frying-pan over a medium heat. Add half the bean curd and cook for 3 minutes a side until golden. Using a slotted spoon transfer to paper towels to drain while frying the remaining bean curd in the same way.

❖ Serve the bean curd on a warm plate with Vinegar Dipping Sauce.

BRAISED BEAN CURD WITH SESAME SEEDS

Tubujorim 2

Braised bean curd is a typical dish of Korean home cooking. Serve braised bean curd as a side dish, accompanied by rice and vegetables, and meat or fish as liked.

SERVES 2-4

2 tbsp Japanese soy sauce
1 tsp sesame oil
1½ garlic cloves, crushed and chopped
2 tsp sugar
¼ tsp chilli powder
2 tsp Crushed Toasted Sesame Seeds (see page 22)
2 spring onions, white and green parts thinly sliced
200g/7oz medium-firm bean curd, cut into 5mm/¼in thick rectangular slices
1½ tbsp vegetable oil
freshly ground black pepper

❖ Mix together the soy sauce, sesame oil, garlic, sugar, chilli powder, sesame seeds and spring onions. Set aside.

❖ Put the bean curd in a single layer between two layers of paper towels. Cover with a plate and put a weight on the plate. Leave for 30 minutes or so.

❖ Heat the vegetable oil in a large frying-pan. Add the bean curd in a single layer and fry for about 1½ minutes a side until browned. Using a slotted spatula, transfer to a large plate. Pour or wipe the oil from the pan.

❖ Return the bean curd to the pan in a single layer. Pour over the soy sauce mixture, partially cover the pan and simmer for 6–7 minutes, turning the bean curd half-way through. Most of the sauce should be absorbed into the bean curd during this time.

❖ Transfer the bean curd to a warm plate and pour over the remaining sauce.

As in other Far Eastern countries, meals in Korea do not finish with a dessert; fresh fruit, of which there is a wonderful, luscious selection – plump strawberries, plums, persimmons, apples – is the most common way of rounding off a meal. However, sweet cakes and other sweetmeats are served for special occasions, such as birthdays, weddings and New Year. Although Korea is surrounded by mighty tea-drinking nations, its people rarely touch it. They do, however, drink copiously of their own versions of teas, made from roasted barley, gingseng and ginger.

BARLEY TEA

Poricha

Poricha is ubiquitous throughout Korea. In winter it is served hot, in summer it is served cold, sweetened with honey or sugar. Poricha has a distinctive, smoky taste, and is quite free of caffeine. Roast barley is available from Korean and Japanese food shops.

MAKES 900ML/1 ½PT

2 tbsp roast barley
900ml/1 ½pt water

❖ Put the roast barley and water into a saucepan and bring to the boil. Lower the heat and simmer the tea until it is as strong as you like it. Strain.

ROLLED SESAME SLICES

Kkaegangjong

These uncooked biscuits are rolled up like a Swiss roll then cut across into slices; this is easiest to do if you use a hot sharp knife.

SERVES 4

50g/2oz white sesame seeds
50g/2oz black sesame seeds
about 65g/2½oz light brown sugar
8 tbsp golden syrup

❖ Heat the white and black sesame seeds in separate dry heavy frying-pans until they just begin to pop.

❖ Gently heat the sugar in the golden syrup, stirring until the sugar has dissolved. Mix half with the white sesame seeds and half with the black sesame seeds.

❖ Spread each mixture out on a sheet of waxed paper. Put another sheet of waxed paper on each and roll out. Remove the top sheets of waxed paper and invert the black sesame seed mixture on to the white sesame seed mixture. Remove the waxed paper now on top. Roll up the sesame seed mixtures firmly, enclosing the black in the white and using the underneath sheet of paper to help you. Leave until cold, then cut into slices.

Rolled Sesame Slices ▶

BISCUIT BOWS

Maejakkwa

These crisp biscuits are very moreish, but if you can resist eating them all soon after they are made they will keep in an air-tight container for several days.

SERVES 4-6

115g/4oz plain flour
1½ tbsp caster sugar
3 tbsp rice wine or dry sherry
vegetable oil for deep-frying
about 115ml/4fl oz clear honey
chopped pine nuts for coating

❖ Stir together the flour and sugar and slowly pour in the rice wine or dry sherry to make a smooth dough; add a little water if necessary. Knead lightly on a floured surface then roll out lightly to a thin rectangle. Cut into 5 x 2.5cm/2 x 1in pieces. Cut a lengthwise slit about 2.5cm/1in long in the centre of each piece. Pull one end of each piece through the slit so the piece resembles a small bow shape.

❖ Heat the oil in a deep-fat fryer to 160°C/330°F. Add the bows and fry for 4–5 minutes until rich golden brown. Remove and drain briefly on a pad of paper towels.

❖ Meanwhile, gently heat the honey (dilute with a little water if the honey is too thick). Dip the bows in the honey to coat, then sprinkle with chopped pine nuts.

Biscuit Bows and Ginger Tea (p125) ▶

GINGER TEA

Saenggangcha

In addition to being a digestive, Saenggangcha is meant to be good for coughs and colds.

MAKES 1 LITRE/1¾PT

3 x 2.5cm/1in pieces of fresh ginger, coarsely chopped
strip of orange peel
4–5 tsp clear honey
ground cinnamon for sprinkling
pine nuts for decorating

❖ Put the ginger, orange peel and honey in a saucepan and add 1 litre/1¾pt water. Bring to the boil, then simmer gently for 15–20 minutes.

❖ Strain the tea and sprinkle a little cinnamon on top. Serve hot or cold with a few pine nuts floating on the surface.

SPICED HONEY CAKES

Yakkwa

In Korea, there are special *yakkwa* moulds for shaping these deep-fried cakes. To get the juice from fresh ginger squeeze a piece of peeled fresh ginger in a taint-free garlic press.

SERVES 4

115g/4oz self-raising flour
1 tsp ground cinnamon
grated zest of ½ lemon
2 tbsp rice wine or dry sherry
2 tbsp clear honey
1 tsp fresh ginger juice
2 tbsp sesame oil
vegetable oil for deep-frying
sesame seeds for coating

❖ Sift the flour and cinnamon into a bowl. Stir in the lemon zest then add the rice wine or sherry, honey, ginger juice and sesame oil and enough water to make a smooth dough. Knead the dough then roll out on a lightly floured surface to about 5mm/¼in thick. Using a 4cm/1½in biscuit cutter, cut into circles.

❖ Heat the vegetable oil in a deep-fat fryer. Add the cakes in batches so they are not crowded, and fry until they rise to the surface and are light golden brown, about 3–5 minutes. Transfer to paper towels to drain. Sprinkle with sesame seeds.

◀ *Spiced Honey Cakes*

GINSENG TEA

Insamcha

Korean ginseng is believed to be the best, and in Korea (and elsewhere) ginseng is purported to cure all manner of ills, from insomnia to impotence. A favourite way of taking ginseng is in the form of a tea.

MAKES 900ML/1½PT

3 slices of red ginseng
1cm/½in piece of fresh ginger, sliced
3 jujubes (Chinese dates), cut into pieces

❖ Put all the ingredients into a saucepan, add 900ml/1½pt water and bring to the boil. Lower the heat, cover and simmer for 1 hour.

❖ Strain into cups. Add pieces of jujube, gingseng and ginger to each cup if liked.

RICE TEA

Sungnyung

When rice is cooked in the traditional way in large pots (although now electric rice cookers are often used) some grain invariably sticks to the bottom of the pot and burns. Once all the non-burnt rice is served, hot water is poured into the pot and boiled. This is then served as a digestive rice tea at the end of the meal. There are many versions of rice tea, and one can be made without first cooking and burning a pot of rice.

MAKES 900ML/1½PT

2 tbsp uncooked long-grain rice
900ml/1½pt boiling water

❖ Put the rice into a small heavy frying-pan and cook over a medium-low heat, stirring, until the rice becomes flecked with dark patches and has a rich nutty aroma.

❖ Tip the rice into a saucepan, add the boiling water, return to the boil then simmer for 1½ minutes. Cover and remove from the heat. Leave for 5 minutes, then strain and serve the tea while still hot.

INDEX